KIDS *STILL* SAY
THE DARNDEST THINGS!

BY ART LINKLETTER

People Are Funny

Kids Say the Darndest Things

The Secret World of Kids

Confessions of a Happy Man

Kids *Still* Say the Darndest Things

Art

Linkletter:

Illustrated by

CHARLES M. SCHULZ

KIDS
Still
SAY
THE
DARNDEST
THINGS!

PUBLISHED BY **BERNARD GEIS ASSOCIATES**
DISTRIBUTED BY RANDOM HOUSE

First Printing

Library of Congress Catalog Number: 61–15781

Manufactured in the United States of America by American Book–Stratford Press, New York

This book is dedicated to the newest generation as exemplified by my grandsons Michael, Dennis, Kevin and Jimmy (in the order of their appearance). I can hardly wait for them to start saying The Darndest Things.
—ART LINKLETTER

Contents

As I Was Saying...

THIS book may remind you of another that I wrote just for fun a few years ago. It was called *Kids Say the Darndest Things*. Any resemblance is quite intentional, because this is a brand new helping of the quips, slips and shockers created by the greatest natural comedians of our day—The Kids.

When *Kids Say* first reached you readers, I had no idea that it would soar up onto the best seller list. What a thrill that was! I watched in a pleased glow as it stayed up there, month after month. I found myself being invited to appear on various occasions, intellectual and otherwise, as Linkletter the Writer.

I began going to autograph parties at bookstores, and I discovered myself making noises like an author. I enjoyed swiveling back in my chair at my Hollywood office and chatting long-distance with my publisher, Bernard Geis, over such authorish things as new editions, Pocket Book reprints, future publishing plans and the like.

All this has been heady and delightful. I've really enjoyed being acclaimed as the Hemingway of the Hopscotch Set. But the truth is that I was more the editor than the author of *Kids Say*. The kids themselves wrote that book, hundreds of kids, a laugh at a time. Then author Arthur sat down, scissors in hand, and strung their ribbons of laughter together like so many paper dolls.

Now comes this sequel to *Kids Say the Darndest Things*. It had to happen, because the kids on my daily "House Party" show seem to have been working with special zest to supply me with funny material. There's a whole new treasure chest of fresh gems, brighter and more sparkling than ever, because kids are getting smarter all the time. But before letting you at them, permit me to slow you up long enough to give you my answer to this question which is asked me so often: "Why have 'The Kids' been such a sure-fire hit on your 'House Party' program for the last seventeen years?"

I think the real answer is: suspense. A kid is a potential keg of dynamite with a short fuse. He's frank and unafraid, and he sees life with an impish focus that is refreshingly honest. Parents sit with fingers crossed while he's talking. Relatives tune in to hear what's *really* going on in their family tree. And just plain people relax to chuckle over bloopers, howlers and boners that are certain to pop up when kids under ten start talking.

One youngster on my program the other day was a little more ambitious than most. "I've been hearing lots of exciting things about this juvenile delinquency thing," he said. "How do you get into it?"

We grownups, of course, are more interested in studying how to get youngsters out of it. One approach is to invite the kids into your home for parties—and they won't be out breaking street lights and stealing hub caps, because they'll be inside breaking floor lamps and raiding the refrigerator. If that sounds a bit too rugged, however, tune in on the kids in these pages as they engage in their time-honored pursuit of life, love, liberty—and smaller kids.

But before you do, I must speak to you seriously for just a moment.

In *Our Town*, Thornton Wilder has his heroine, Emily, say to her mother, "Oh, Mama, just look at me one minute as though you really saw me. Let's look at one another. Do any human beings ever realize life while they live it—every, every minute? Oh, earth, you're too wonderful for anyone to realize you." And that's what I think when I see my youngsters growing up, the precious moments of childhood racing by. How can I squeeze every last second of fun, excitement and sweetness out of those strange little creatures who are ours for so short a time?

The next time you talk to a little child, look deeply into his eyes. Don't just glance at him, or over him, or through him. Look straight through those wide-open, unguarded "eye-portals" into his mind. You'll feel an answering, almost forgotten stirring in your own mind. You'll be in touch with innocence and the long ago. Do it—for it's one of the best things in life.   ART LINKLETTER

Home, Sweet Home

Home is the very center of a child's fascinating world. Naturally, he's just bursting with information about what's going on around the house. That's why parents so often discover to their chagrin that their child is a walking arsenal of explosive tidbits on such supposedly private topics as what Daddy really thinks of his boss, what Mommy does for fun, and many other family secrets that would titillate their friends and neighbors.

Pumping other people's kids for inside gossip is a fine old tradition among curious folk generally. On my show, I just carry on this grand old custom—pumping away at the kids and passing all their juicy revelations on to you!

Would you like to hear a recipe for a happy marriage? I heard one when I asked a little boy, "What do your folks do for fun?" He told me: "My mom drinks beer, my dad watches television—and then they take bubble baths together." You can imagine the delighted roar that went up from the audience at this vivid mental picture of sudsy togetherness—and the ribbing that this boy's blushing parents took later from friends and relatives over their good clean fun.

Talking to the youngsters before the show each day, I can usually tell which ones will be liveliest and least inhibited when we're on the air.

They're the impatient ones. They kick aimlessly, scratch everywhere and fidget incessantly. They blurt out answers before a question is finished, and endlessly ask when something new will happen. They are the self-assured leaders, never concerned in the slightest over what others think of them. And when they finally sit before my audience of ten million, they react with the same easy confidence as if they were home in their own playrooms. It's amazing.

The question most asked me at parties is usually whispered in a confidential manner. It's this: "What would you do if a youngster on your show said something really bad?"

I can answer that one right out loud. In seventeen years, no youngster has said anything "really bad"—because they have no thoughts or intentions that could be interpreted as naughty. Shocking things, yes. But bad, never. To paraphrase an old saying, "Think no evil, speak no evil."

In the mind of a normal six-year-old, all of Nature is simply natural. Here's what I mean:

A mother had sent her little son to a progressive camp. Coming to visit him, she found he was quite excited about having gone swimming in the camp pool.

"But how did you do that?" she asked. "I forgot to pack your bathing trunks for you."

"I went in naked."

"Did the girls go in naked, too?"

"Oh, no," was his answer, "they wore bathing caps."

If we'd had a laugh meter on stage, we'd have blown a fuse or two the day that seven-year-old Danny told his ver-

sion of his father's life as a man of medicine. First Danny told me he wanted to be a doctor, too, so I asked, "What would you do if I came to you with a bad cold?"

He drew away from me as though I were teeming with germs, and said hastily: "I'd leave. I wouldn't want to catch it!"

"What does your mother think of your dad being a doctor?"

"It kind of upsets her."

"In what way?"

"Well, Dad gets a call at night, and Mom wishes he'd stay in bed with her instead of getting up and going to bed with some patient."

After some of the disclosures kids make on my "House Party" show you'd think they'd head straight for the Mexican border instead of home. They seem to have no fears whatever about pulling up the shades on all sorts of family shenanigans. The supposedly dull drudgery of being a housewife, for example, was challenged by an enthusiastic little girl who wanted to be one "because they have so much fun sitting around drinking highballs."

"How do you know?" I asked.

She leaned forward with a confidential air: "I know a housewife who does it all the time."

"Who's that?" I asked—but a gasp from a woman in the audience reminded my little informant that we were being overheard.

"It's a secret," she sighed. "My mom said if I told you, she'd whack me good when I got home."

When you were a child, did you ever live dangerously by blowing up a hunk of bubble gum until it exploded all over your face? That's how I felt when an innocent question blew up on me. All I asked was, "How did your folks meet?" This was the answer: "In a store in New Jersey, and after they had some dates they went to different cities. Then Mommy's lawyer wrote Daddy and told him he ought to marry her, so they did." Somehow I think that one was a family joke that "little pitchers" picked up, but I'll never know for sure.

I once heard a famous private investigator say that no one leads so blameless a life that he can afford to have all his activities known to the public. And imagine how you'd feel if you suddenly learned that there'd been a wiretap on your phone, or worse yet, a microphone hidden away in your home. Wouldn't you turn just a shade crimson at the thought, wondering what secrets and confidences were overheard? There is such a hidden mike in millions of homes throughout this land

of ours. It's called a child, and it picks up everything within earshot with high fidelity. Here's a girl tuned in on her father: "My daddy fixes tv sets for a living."

"What if he finds there's nothing wrong with a set?"
"He charges 'em anyway."

Here's a boy attuned to the secret misgivings of a professional man:

"My daddy is a doctor—an anaesthetist."
"What's that?"
"He's a man who puts people to sleep in hospitals."
"Then what?"
"Then he hopes they wake up."

Letter writers by the thousands are always asking how children are selected to appear on the "House Party" show. Usually the writer is a proud parent or grandparent whose offspring is full of bright sayings around the house. Actually, during the regular school season, we depend on the Los Angeles school system to supply our guests.

Teachers have several different ways of choosing which children to send. Sometimes a child will frankly admit he was chosen because he's teacher's pet. And sometimes a long-suffering teacher will pick the kid at the bottom end of her popularity scale, so that she can enjoy a peaceful day without him!

The real wonder of my television interviews is that the kids can be so outgoing and relaxed under circumstances that have often caused veteran screen actors to gulp and freeze into silence. There they sit, facing four hundred strangers in the studio audience, with lights glaring down at them, red-eyed cameras pushing in at them, a microphone under their noses, and Linkletter asking questions. Sometimes there's an added menace on the scene, in the person of a tense, uneasy, head-shaking parent. Of course the other kind of parent, the beaming, confident type, can be a great comfort to the tinier ones.

For sheer confidence and mastery of the entire situation, I can't recall anyone who topped ten-year-old Kirk, a fast-talking boy with a Hollywood columnist's instinct for dishing up gossip. I asked him to describe his family. He took an enormous breath and started off:

"My mom's a Texas Democrat with dyed red hair. My dad's a Louisiana Democrat with black hair and a few white spots. I don't know what my grandma is, but I do know she still eats with the false teeth she got when she was twenty-nine. I've got an aunt who has a whole lot of money. I know because she paid cash for her house. I think that describes my family."

"Yes, that takes care of them pretty well! But how about you?"

"I'm going to be in the Navy."

"Why?"

"When you die, you die clean."

"Will you be a single or a married sailor?"

"Single, because if you're married and come home with the

paycheck and you doze off, when you wake up your wife's got that check and spent it already."

"I imagine your mother is a little alarmed at our discussion so far. Did she give you any instructions before you left home?"

"No, she said it was no use, I'd just forget them anyway."

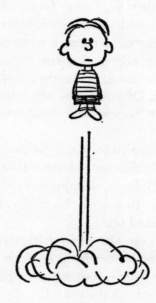

"Does she ever get angry with you?"

"You bet."

"What's the first sign?"

"She starts the countdown."

"How does that work?"

"She counts from ten down to one."

"And then what?"

"I don't know. I'm gone from the launching pad before she ever gets that far!"

During summer vacations and holiday weeks, our kids come to us from private schools and such groups as the YMCA, YWCA and Boy Scouts.

Being on our show isn't a glorified kind of hookey-playing. It's planned as a learning experience, including a tour of TV City where the youngsters find out how their favorite programs are created.

I've often wondered what the kids make of it all as they wander through the huge studios, all cluttered with equipment, so I talked it over with a group of our Boy Scouts recently.

I told the Scouts, "We feel that the tour through CBS is very worthwhile for you, so let's see what you learned today." Here's how they answered:

* The cameras cost fourteen thousand dollars apiece.

* Most programs are taped and not live.

* The director's never supposed to get mad.

* The musicians on this show match quarters after rehearsal, and the piano player always wins.

    (That last boy was right about the piano player!)

Children leap from ambition to ambition like mountain goats. It's only natural that all boys will want to be firemen at some stage in their lives, because kids love excitement, glamour and danger. But there are other ambitions well worth noting at the earliest ages, because they give parents a clue to the child's developing personality.

Ten-year-old Janice wanted to be a zoologist.

"What does a zoologist do?"

"Classifies animals."

"That's right. How would you classify me?"

She studied me intently, and then put me in my place:

"You're a mammal with a backbone, an anthropoid, human, warm-blooded man and you have a big nose!"

❖   ❖   ❖

What do you want to be?

A businessman and a bachelor like my father.

How can your dad be a bachelor?

I don't know; he's the tax collector, and I've heard people call him something like that.

Occasionally it's fun to ask the kids what they *wouldn't* like to be. Here's an almost unbearably vivid picture of why one young man has decided against a career in medicine. I'd asked him the question, and he made a wry face as he said:

"I wouldn't want to be a surgeon."

"Why not?"

"Oh, they have to go through hours of taking out people's hearts and livers and gizzards, while other people stand around and watch. And sometimes something *bad* happens."

"Like what?"

"Like when the doctor says 'oops!' and pulls the sheet over their head."

❧ CHAPTER II ❧

My Mommy Says

THERE is a ritual that all mothers seem to follow when they are grooming one of their young ones to appear on my show. First comes a good scrubbing, a Sunday-morning-style washing of tiny hands, faces, ears and necks. Then comes the brainwashing, to cleanse the child's mind of all those family secrets that mother doesn't want blurted out in front of ten million

23

strangers. The way I foil these maternal brainwashers is as effective as it is sneaky. I simply ask the child what his mother told him *not* to say, and out it comes! After all, he's been rehearsed in it so often that he has it letter-perfect.

A ten-year-old boy sits before me with that faraway look in his eyes, so I move in with that old dependable secret-loosener:

"What did your mother tell you not to say?"

He reacts instantly, as though I've pressed the magic button on his mental tape recorder:

"She said not to tell you that Dad calls her 'lard bottom.' "

The audience roars with laughter, and I'm left to wonder for a fleeting moment whether the boy's mother will warm *his* bottom later for drawing national attention to hers.

Over the years I've discovered that many parents go through a complete emotional cycle, from delirious joy to soul-searching doubt, after their child reveals he's been chosen to be on my show. The first announcement sends the parents running for the telephone to boast to all their friends about the young performer in their midst. Letters are fired off to relations all over the country, so everyone will be sure to see the family's pride in action.

Now Mom and Dad listen carefully to my show, making mental notes of the questions I ask, and imagining how their own child might reply. This is when that first burst of joy starts to fade, and the murmurings of doubt begin.

Suppose their son tells about the cocktail party they had, the one that ended when the neighborhood busybody called the police? What if he blabs about how they've been hiding from the installment man? What if he reveals that his dad thinks his boss is a fatheaded skinflint?

Suddenly it dawns on them that their boy has seen and

heard enough around the house to blast the place right off its foundations! So the brainwashing starts in earnest, and everyone the child has ever heard criticized is suddenly elevated to sainthood. It's a courageous, rear-guard battle that the parents put up, but defeat lies ahead of them. They're always outflanked by that question that reveals what they've tried hardest to hide. Here are some more of the family secrets that kids were told *not* to reveal:

❖ My mother said not to tell you that she's forty-five years old and aging.

❖ I'm not supposed to talk about my uncle, who just hangs around the house and reads the racing form all day.

On and on go the revelations, including many that the parents hadn't even thought to warn the child about:

❖ My mom's mad at Dad because he lost half his paycheck playing poker last night.

❖ My mom had such a hangover yesterday that she had to call up and make an excuse instead of teaching Sunday School.

❖ My dad thinks half the judges in this town are crooks, and he ought to know because he's a lawyer.

❖ My dad's a minister, and he says our congregation is so tight it squeaks.

Fathers think it's great fun to prime their kids with a gag or two.

Charles, do you have any instructions from home?

Daddy told me to ask you, Why don't Jewish people ever get jailed?

All right, you've got me. Why don't Jewish people get jailed?

Because they eat lox.

❖   ❖   ❖

Any instructions from Dad?

❖ Daddy taught me a joke to tell you.

Let's hear it.

Roses are red, violets are blue, if skunks had a college, they'd call it P.U.!

❖   ❖   ❖

Any instructions from Mother?

❖ My mother said to act natural, except that I should be polite.

❖ My mother said I mustn't tell any of my dad's jokes because they're too dirty.
   Like what?
   Oh, you wouldn't understand them anyway.

❖ My mother said not to tell any fibs.
   She's here today, isn't she?
   Yes. That's her there in the front row with my brother Craig.
   How old is Craig?
   Mom told the ushers he's twelve to get him in here—but he's really only ten!

❖ I was told to just act normal.
   What's normal?
   I think it's 98.6.
   I guess I walked right into that one!

CHAPTER III

Classroom Comedians

Evidently I am now the world's champion collector of the funny sayings of school kids. It's a wonderful hobby, but I must confess that it wasn't really my idea. It all began when my first book about kids was published, and everyone across the country discovered that one A. Linkletter in Hollywood enjoyed kid jokes. Next thing I knew, people were sending me all *their* favorites—and my office became the child joke capital of America. Now the joke's on me, I'm happy to say, because I can scarcely get through my mail in the morning without going on a laughing jag.

While I'm confessing, I might as well face up to the obvious and admit that schoolteachers discovered long before I did that kids say the darndest things. Classroom bloopers and examination boners have been delighting teachers ever since the days when Socrates was pounding a little knowledge into Plato's head back in ancient Greece.

The blooperizing of knowledge goes on and on, so I'd like to share some of my classroom favorites with you, as sent in by teachers and readers.

Not long ago a teacher asked her first-grade class who Nikita Khrushchev was. Here were the answers:

❖ I know he isn't a cowboy because I've never seen him on television.

❖ He's a wrestler.

❖ I never heard of him, but I know he doesn't live on our street.

❖ ❖ ❖

A first-grader came home from school asking questions about a man named Richard Stands.

"I never heard of anybody named Richard Stands," said his mother.

"He must be somebody important," the kid persisted, "because when we salute the Flag, we say, 'I pledge allegiance to the Flag of the United States of America and to the Republic for Richard Stands.' "

❖ ❖ ❖

"I won a prize in kindergarten today," a boy boasted to his mother. "Teacher asked me how many legs a hippopotamus has, and I said 'three.' "

"Three?" said his mother. "How on earth could you have won the prize?"

"I came the closest," the boy said.

❖ ❖ ❖

Here's a delightful story that came from a third-grade classroom on the West Coast:

All the pupils were asked to draw pictures of what they wanted to be when they grew up. One boy drew himself as a plane pilot. Another drew himself at the wheel of a fire engine. But a little girl turned in a blank piece of paper. When teacher asked why, the girl explained: "I want to be married—but I don't know how to *draw* it."

❖ ❖ ❖

A teacher in a farming community in the Midwest assigned each of her pupils to write a brief composition about their fathers. Here were the essays handed in:

❖ My pop is tops because he helped get our parish plastered.
❖ My dad is a farmer. He smells like a cow. When I come in and smell a cow in the house, I know my dad is home and I'm glad.

❖ My dad brings me up right because he don't want I should be a jovial delinquent.

Some of the most charming one-sentence compositions come, as you might expect, from the youngest children. Here are some ideas that are almost poetry, from kids barely old enough to write:

❖ Cats are for dogs to chase.

❖ Ears are to wiggle.

❖ A door is to answer.

❖ A face is a thing that holds your head and hair in place.

❖ Mountains are a place where it's hard to go up but easy to come down.

❖ A hat is a thing to tip and say, "How do you do."

❖ The world is where you jump up in the air and always come down again.

❖ A package is something to say, "Yoo hoo! Look what I got!"

❖   ❖   ❖

The Great Emancipator was famed for the brevity of his writings, but he could never have surpassed the nine-year-old who wrote this:

"Abe Lincoln was born. Then he became a boy. Then he became a man. Then he became President. Then he was shot. The End."

❖   ❖   ❖

Here is a little girl's essay on "People":

"People are composed of girls and boys, also men and women. Boys are no good until they grow up and get married. Men who don't get married are no good either. Girls are young women who will be ladies when they graduate. Boys are an awful bother. They want everything they see except soap. If I had my way, half of the boys in the world would be girls, and the other half dolls. My ma is a woman and my pa is a man. A woman is a grown-up girl with children. My pa is such a nice man I guess he must have been a little girl when he was a little boy."

❖   ❖   ❖

After a class toured the White House, the teacher asked the students to write their impressions of the visit. One boy wrote: "I was especially glad to have this opportunity to visit my future home."

Here's an assortment of the kind of answers teachers get when pupils are hazy on the questions:

What do you think of the world situation?
   It's round.
Who was Joan of Arc?
   Noah's wife.
What was George Washington known as?
   George.
What is it when I say, "I love you, you love me, he loves me?"
   One of those triangles where somebody gets shot.

Knowledge and learning suffer the same kind of merry mayhem at the hands of Sunday School pupils. Let's look at some of the more confusing pages of the Kids Revised Version of the Good Book:

"Johnny, who defeated the Philistines?"
"I don't know. If they don't play the Dodgers, I don't keep track of them."

❖   ❖   ❖

"What vision did Saul have on the Road to Damascus?"
After a long silence, a boy spoke up timidly:
"Twenty-twenty?"

❖   ❖   ❖

A veteran Sunday School instructor who saves such things sent me this assortment of classroom boners:

❖ The Bible is against Bigamy when it says that no man can serve two masters.

❖ The tower of Babel was the place where Solomon kept his wives.

❖ The Crusaders had many hardships, and many of them died of Salvation.

❖ Blessed are the weak in heart, for they shall see God.

❖ The Eskimos are God's frozen people.

❖   ❖   ❖

A teacher told her class to think of a Bible story and draw it, so one boy handed in a sketch of a long sports car with three faces peering out.

"What Bible story is that?" she asked.

"That's the Lord driving Adam and Eve out of the Garden of Eden," the boy said.

Examination bloopers have brightened many a long dreary hour at grading time for teachers. Here are a few that have become classics over the years:

❖ One of the chief uses of water is to save people from drowning in.

❖ A stethoscope is a spyglass for looking into people's chests with your ears.

❖ An optimist is a man who looks after your eyes. A pessimist takes care of your feet.

❖ If you want to see a mosque in Europe, you go to Moscow.

❖ The cold at the North Pole is so great that the towns there are not inhabited.

❖ Christians are only allowed one wife. This is called monotony.

❖ A sincere friend is one who says nasty things to your face instead of behind your back.

❖ Dust is mud with the juice squeezed out.

And here's a closer that any parent will understand.
"Cleanliness is next to—what?"
"Impossible."

❦ CHAPTER IV ❦

The Kindly Young Philosophers

CHILDREN are nutshell philosophers. They say things straight out and straight at you in a very few words. It's a headlong, pell-mell rush for the truth that leaves many an adult in a mild state of shock, his eyebrows arching upwards.

A ten-year-old nutsheller gave me his view of life's biggest problem in just three words: "Getting through it."

A girl of nine summed up the feminine life in the space of a telegram:

"When you're young like me, you hate boys. When you're grown, you're trying to get boys, and when you're older, you're trying to keep the boys you've got."

Try tuning in on your child's mind, and you'll soon discover that he's been tuning in on *you*—listening to your opinions on everything from love and marriage to the chances for peace in the Middle East. The fun comes when the child does some thinking on his own, and figures out what *he* would do about the problems of the world.

An international expert sat before me recently, a little boy from Mexico with a brilliant smile and shining black eyes. He'd been thinking about the world lately and had decided to tell me his new ambition:

"I want to be the Presidente."

"What would you do first as our Presidente?"

"There'd be no more wars," he promised.

"How would you manage that?"

"More siestas for everybody!"

Four eleven-year-old military cadets had varying ideas on how best to keep peace in the world.

❖ Fight back.

❖ Take the best men out of all the armies and put them in a super army.

❖ Give tv sets to all the armies, so they'll be too happy watching to fight.

❖ Don't nobody start nothin'!

❖　❖　❖

Ever hear of a Spwinkle Man? Neither had I until I met Nathan.

What does your father do, Nathan?

He woiks.

What does he woik at?

He builds wockets.

What do you want to be when you grow up?

A spwinkle man.

What would you do all day?
  Just spwinkle.
What if you were an animal?
  I'd be a wion.
Why?
  Because I never was one.

Suppose the world of parents and kids were turned upside down for a while, and the kids were raising the grownups. How would they change us? It's an intriguing idea, and it's surprising how much thought the average youngster has given to this dream of transforming his elders into ideal parents. Here's what a typical group of school kids said when I asked them to tell how they'd improve their parents:

❖ I'd have them raise my allowance from fifty cents to a dollar a week. Dad would take me to all the ball games, and Mother would do more work around the house instead of putting it on my shoulders.

❖ I think my dad should start dieting and Mother should stop.

❖ I wish my mom would stop telling my dad that he's fat, and I wish he'd stop telling her that she's too skinny.

There are days when my young guests become so serious and philosophical that they sound like scholars. Recently four eleven-year-olds were so sober-sided that I tried to lighten our talk by reaching into my bag of sure-fire questions. I came up with this one: "Who has a secret?"

The atmosphere changed immediately as these secrets came tumbling out:

❖ I want to be a biologist, and the first bug I'd like to dissect is my sister.

❖ My secret is that my dad hates to drink beer, and what makes it a secret is that he works for the Regal Pale brewery.

❖ My sister is out in the audience—and she's about to have a baby any minute.

❖ I have a crush on my man teacher, and I'd just die if he ever found out.
Well, you've all come to the right place to keep a secret!

All kids have some simple kind of philosophy. More often than not, it's a common saying they've heard that makes sense to them.

What's your philosophy of life?

He who laughs last, laughs best.

How does that work?

My brother's always laughing at me, and one night I was sent away from the table because I was playing with the fruit salad instead of eating it, and my brother laughed.

Then what?

I laughed last as I went to my room, because I didn't like what we were having for dinner anyway.

❖   ❖   ❖

Nine-year-old Mark had life all figured out like this:

"When you're young, your parents support you. When

you're middle-aged, you support yourself. And when you're old, the Government supports you."

❖ ❖ ❖

Have you heard the expression, "Life begins at forty"?
Yes, but it's not true. God doesn't make anybody begin at forty.

❖ ❖ ❖

If you had your life to live over, what would you do?
I'd skip the childhood diseases.
What have you had?
Measles and chicken pops.

One of the most refreshing things about talking to kids is that they see life through the other end of the telescope. I've always loved the story of the four-year-old boy who was fascinated by airplanes. Every day he rushed out to see one flying past. At last the day came when he had his first ride in one. He was very excited. But ten minutes after take-off, he turned to his mother with a puzzled look and asked, "When do we start to get smaller?"

Here are some more child's-eye-views of life:

What's the biggest problem in growing up?

Having to live with your parents and keep them up to date.

❖ ❖ ❖

What's the big news around your house?

Mom's getting a baby in May.

What do you want, a boy or a girl?

Oh, we don't care. We're just going to let the doctor surprise us.

❖ ❖ ❖

What's the worst thing about being ten years old?

Your friends are all getting too old to go to a birthday party.

❖   ❖   ❖

Who has more vanity, Everett—girls or boys?
Girls.
Why?
Boys wear shirts for a whole week, but girls change sometimes.

❖   ❖   ❖

What's an ideal husband like, Evelyn?
He shaves, lets his wife spend his money, and isn't a bachelor.

There are times when a child will express an idea of real wisdom in a beautifully apt way. I'll never forget six-year-old Kathy's definition of a good friend:

"It's somebody who remembers your birthday, even when you forget hers."

❖   ❖   ❖

Where is the wishbone in the human animal?
Under the hat.

An eight-year-old had been doing a lot of thinking about the goings on in the Garden of Eden, and he'd reached some rather original conclusions. I asked him: "Who's the smartest man in the world?"
"The first man born—Adam."
"Why was he so smart?"
"He made a woman out of his stomach and decided he didn't like it."
"What's so smart about that?"
"Now the women have to do it!"

Kids are under a constant barrage of "do's" and "don'ts" about their conduct from both parents and Sunday School teachers, so it's not surprising that they have vivid ideas about good and evil.
I asked six-year-old Tommy: "What makes boys good or bad?"
"Good boys say their prayers," he assured me.
"That's right. Which prayer do you say?"
"That's the whole trouble," he sighed. "I don't say any."

❖   ❖   ❖

What's your idea of the worst thing in life?
Greed.
What do you mean?

There are so many greedy, greedy people trying to get all the money.
Do you know any people like that?
Yes, me.

❖   ❖   ❖

Here's a contemporary version of the Good Samaritan:
"What's the best deed you ever did?"
"I helped a friend who was being beat up."
"How did you help him?"
"I yelled at the guys who were beating him, and they came over and beat me."

CHAPTER V

Shaggy Dogs and Elephants

Oᴺᴇ of the more impressive members of the Linkletter menagerie is on public display at the Los Angeles Zoo. Now please don't go rushing down there to look through the monkey cages for a Linkletter name plate. I'm not talking about a blood relative. The creature I'm referring to is an adopted elephant from India named Gita. She's just a baby, and we love every ton of her.

Gita is only the latest of a long series of widely assorted creatures that have taken up residence with our family at one time or another. We actually kept her in our back yard for a while. I suppose she did cause talk among the neighbors when the wind shifted, but no one ever actually stopped by to suggest that I trade her for something more fashionable, like a poodle. Besides, my long-lived "People Are Funny" show conditioned the neighbors to shut their eyes to *anything* happening on our street.

It was great fun to have Gita round the place, and I enjoyed

casually informing people that I had to go home to feed our
elephant. But eventually we had to bid her farewell. I had
promised the children of India who had given her to me that
I would make a present of Gita to the children of Los Angeles.
So there she is now at the Zoo, the only performing Linkletter
ever to be happy working for peanuts.

I'm sure most parents who've had experience will agree
that a pet can be a wonderful influence in a child's life. Fun
and companionship? There's plenty of that between a boy and
his pet, but there are other benefits too. Having a pet and
caring for its needs and happiness is a marvelous way for a
child to learn responsibility and a feeling for other living creatures in the world.

As much as I approve of pets, I can still sympathize with
harassed, overworked mothers who wonder if they can cope
with both child *and* pet. I asked one four-year-old on the show
if he had any pets, and he said:

"I used to have a cat."

"What happened to it?"

"He 'went' in one corner of my sandbox, and I 'went' in the other, and Mommy said she'd have to get rid of one of us."

A boy who had two dogs told me he was certain they talked to each other by wiggling their ears and tails, so I asked him:

"What do dogs have to talk about?"

"When you see two dogs standing around talking," he said, "they're saying, 'Hey! Let's go chase a car!' "

❖   ❖   ❖

What's the bravest thing you ever did?

I saved my cat from strangling to death.

How did you do that?

I didn't give him some chicken bones.

❖ ❖ ❖

Any pets at home?

We had two bunnies named Felix and Peter. Mother thought we were safe—but Peter turned out to be a Dorothy and now we have ten more bunnies.

❖ ❖ ❖

Any pets?

Two ducks named Jim and Bob. Jim's the mama.

❖ ❖ ❖

What's your dog's name?

Shorty.

What kind of dog is Shorty?

He's a lavatory retriever.

❖ ❖ ❖

If you could choose any pet from the zoo, what would you pick?

A rattlesnake.

What would your mother think of that?
She'd like it.
What makes you so sure?
Because that's the only way left she can get rid of the mice in the house.

Whenever I ask the kids if their dogs have pedigrees, they give me a remarkable variety of answers. They hardly ever know what a pedigree *is;* but their imaginative little minds readily suggest what a pedigree *might* be.

Here are some typical answers to the question: "Does your dog have a pedigree?"

❖ No, we're Lutherans.

❖ Yes, she has three of them—one to keep her from rabies, one from worms and one from puppies.

❖ Of course not! He's a boy.

❖ She had nine puppies in one year so they took her pedigree out.

Seven-year-old Leo liked animals so much that he said he wanted to be a farmer when he grew up.

"What's the most important thing to remember on a farm?" I asked him.

"Don't milk a bull!"

One sure way to set the wheels going around in a child's imagination is to ask him what animal he'd like to be. More often than not, his answer will give you an insight into his own private dreams and fancies. Being a funny, absurd animal like a kangaroo may appeal to him, or he may wish instead to be a huge, powerful teacher-eater like a tiger.

Speaking of kangaroos, how would you describe one? A five-year-old did it quite well for me recently when he said that a kangaroo is "like a great big mouse, with a pocket in its stomach."

A six-year-old girl with her eye on that practical pouch told me she would like to be a kangaroo "so I could carry my notebook, a toothbrush and a piece of cake."

Occasionally I'm properly humbled by the fact that a five-year-old's reasoning can be superior to mine. I asked little Wayne what animal he'd like to be, and he said:

"A cat—so I could eat rats."

"But wouldn't they taste terrible?" I protested.

"Not if you were a cat!"

❖   ❖   ❖

What animal would you like to be, Richard?

A bull, because my mother says I'm full of it.

What's your mother like?

She's not a regular mother. She makes missiles.

How about brothers and sisters in your family?

Mom says she's all through making those, because I'm enough for anybody.

What does your dad say about that?

He says anything my mom wants is okay with him, and he really means it because my mom always wins all the arguments.

❖ ❖ ❖

What animal would you like to be, Michael?
A monkey.
Why?
Because it would be lots of fun to have a tail.
How do monkeys look?
Just like us little boys, except they have fur on themselves.

❖ ❖ ❖

A six-year-old told me he'd like to be a bird more than anything in the world.
Why do you want to be a bird?
Because you can fly anywhere you want to, and you never have to stop, not even to go to the bathroom.

❖ ❖ ❖

What animal would you be?
A seal.
Why?
Because I'd like to go swimming, eat fish and clap my flippers.
Seals have whiskers. Would you like some?
I sure would.
Why do you suppose that seals have whiskers?
Because they don't shave.

CHAPTER VI

Heavenly Daze

SUNDAY School kids enjoy those magnificent Old Testament stories of Adam and Eve, Noah and his Ark, and brave little David standing up to the giant Goliath. Even the smallest boys and girls can feel close to Jesus, with His love for little children just like themselves.

Of course, being the innocents that they are, kids in Sunday School occasionally come away from class with ideas that the teacher never intended. That's where much of the fun of this chapter comes in. But it's also true that the trusting faith of a child can sometimes reach as deeply into religious truth as the mind of any adult.

I've never forgotten the boy who told me his favorite Bible story:

"It's the one about Jesus being born."

"Why do you like that one?"

"Because I feel sorry for boys and girls who have no parents, and when Jesus was born, He became the Father of everyone who has no mother or dad."

Certainly God must be very real in the mind of a girl who had an unusual question for me:

"Mr. Linkletter, are they watching us in heaven on tv?"

"Why do you ask that?"

"Because I want God to hear us."

"Well, I'm sure He's listening, so you go right ahead and tell Him what you want to."

"Could he come down on Saturday night for chicken dinner?"

There was laughter from the grownups at the idea of Our Lord sitting down to a roast chicken supper with the girl's family, but it was gentle laughter, for their hearts were touched.

Six-year-old Jackie told me his favorite Bible story:

"The one where Jesus died for all our sins."

"Why do you like that one?"

"Because I sin all the time."

"You do? How?"

He regarded me sadly and confessed:

"I'm a cookie stealer."

We Linkletters have always been great believers in Sunday School. Every one of our five little Links has attended regularly, all the way through high school. After high school we felt they were old enough to decide for themselves where and when they would attend church.

We never insisted on any particular church, because we found through the years that certain Sunday Schools would be more attractive to the youngsters, due to the gold stars they gave, the picnics or games they organized, or the availability of boy friends and girl friends for after-hours fun. What we did insist on was regular attendance, so they would have a thorough education in the meaning and importance of religion.

The younger a child is, the merrier his confusion over theology seems to be. The difference between the earthly and the saintly baffles many a tiny Sunday Schooler, who finds it just as easy to believe in the Easter Bunny as John the Baptist.

"What's your favorite Bible story?"

"Humpty Dumpty."

"How does it go?"

"There was this egg that fell off the wall and he prayed, but even Heaven couldn't put him back together again."

"Are you sure that's in the Bible?"

"Sure! It's right after Little Bo-Peep!"

❖ ❖ ❖

Seven-year-old Benny was bouncing up and down with excitement as he told me his favorite Bible story about David and Goliath:

"David went to the brook and got seven pebbles, and he put one in his slingshot. Then you know what? He whirled it around and around his head and threw it and hit this great big giant right between the eyes—and the giant fell down dead!"

"What does that story teach us?" I asked.

He sat there thinking for a moment, and then said, "Duck!"

❖   ❖   ❖

Here's a moral-with-a-twist to the story of Noah and his sea-going menagerie. I asked a five-year-old what Noah did, and he said:

"He took all the married animals on a boat and left the bachelors behind."

"What does that story teach us?"

"Always be married—and you won't be left behind on a boat ride."

❖   ❖   ❖

The youngsters sometimes have a different outlook on the

way a Sunday School operates than the church officials might suspect.

"George, what do you want to be?"

"A Sunday School teacher."

"Why?"

"Because you only work one day a week!"

Church music comes in for its share of misinterpretation, too. Small voices are often singing lustily along with words that might startle the congregation if they were clearly heard. I asked a five-year-old what her favorite Sunday School hymn was, and she cheerfully replied: "Jesus, wash my skin away." She reminded me of the boy who came home from a church picnic, and said they'd sung a picnic song called "We Can Sing, though Full We Be." His parents learned later that the hymn was actually "Weak and Sinful though We Be."

You've heard of the King James Version, the Revised Standard Version, and all the others of the Bible. There must also be a Suburban Version, judging from one girl's ideas about life in the Garden of Eden.

"What story do you like best?"

"Adam and Eve."

"What happened to them?"

"They were bad and God sentenced them to work."

"He did? What kind of work?"

"They had to clean the swimming pool every day."

A seven-year-old miss was also fond of the Adam and Eve story, so I asked her:

"What did Eve do?"

"She ate the poison apple and God threw her out of heaven."

"Then what?"

"She went to the hospital and had two children named Cain and Mabel."

And here's a new way to look at Adam's fall from grace, as seen through the eyes of a cautious seven-year-old boy. I asked him:

"What does the story of Adam and Eve teach you?"

"If a naughty girl tempts you to do something bad," he said, "don't do it while God is watching!"

Heaven sounded so good to one boy that he revealed he'd decided to become a preacher.

"What kind of preacher?" I asked.

"A Baptist one."

"Why a Baptist?"

" 'Cause I want to make sure I get into heaven."

"What makes you so sure that Baptists get into heaven?"

"Because St. Peter is one—and he's right there at the gate!"

Sunday Schoolers are utterly fascinated by the story of Jonah's adventures with the whale, and they fascinate me when Jonah floats into the conversation.

"So your favorite story is Jonah and the Whale. What does that story teach us?"

"People make whales sick."

"What's your favorite story?"
"Jonah inside the whale."
"What does that story teach us?"
"If you're ever swallowed by a whale, build a fire and stay warm until the whale sneezes, then you'll be out."
(Something tells me that boy knows his Disney better than his Good Book.)

If there's such a thing as a Biblical shaggy dog story, I think I heard one from a mixed-up five-year-old.
"Do you have a favorite Bible story?"
"Uh huh. Noah and his Ark."
"Who was Noah?"
"A fellow who owned a dog."
"What do you mean?"
"Well, that's the story—Noah and his Ark."
"You mean you think the Ark is a dog?"
"No. It's the *sound* his doggie makes."

All of us have our own ideas about what Heaven might be like. I suppose most people envision it as the artists of the Middle Ages have taught us—a place of immense splendor with pearly gates and complete with immense groups of winged angels in white robes.

Seven-year-old Sally had her own ideas when I asked her what heaven was like. She told me the following very succinct definition of heaven:

"It's a great big round gold dome with three lines of people waiting to get in—Catholics, Lutherans and Americans."

Here is a down-to-earth sermon from a seven-year-old. I asked him:

"What did God do?"

"He invented the world, and houses, and wood, and rocks, and steel, and spiders, and food—"

"Wait a minute. What if we had no God?"

He looked at me thoughtfully and said:

"We'd be in a mess."

Earlier in this chapter, we met the charming little girl who wanted God to come down for chicken dinner. I'd like to tell you one more of my favorites, showing how close a child can feel to his Maker:

A little boy ran into the house and told his mother, "I've just been outside playing ball with God."

"That's ridiculous," his mother said. "You shouldn't say such things."

"But I did too play ball with God," the boy said.

"How could you do that?"

"I just throw the ball up in the air—and God throws it back to me."

CHAPTER VII

Tribal Warfare

Bᴿᴇᴀᴛʜᴇs there a boy with soul so dead, who never to himself has said: "Some day I'll catch that sister of mine where Mom can't hear her yell, and then she'll find out what I *really* think of her. *Pow!* And we'll be even for life!"

What makes an otherwise wonderful, lovable kid turn into a schemer and plotter of sweet revenges when he thinks of his sister? What transforms a charming and adorable young lady into an avenging harpie who swoops down on her younger brother and clobbers him every chance she gets?

Parents may despair over all the battling, but kids just accept it as an everyday fact of life. Here's a perfectly honest reaction of a nine-year-old to the question: "What's your family like?"

"It's just a normal family," he said. "My big brother thinks he's king of the world, my big sister blames everything that goes wrong on me, and my little brother's a stinker."

Equally honest was an eleven-year-old boy telling me about his sister:

"She's the kind of girl who'd punch me in the mouth if I said anything bad about her."

"But what's she *really* like?" I persisted.

"I guess she's all right on the inside," he admitted. "But I get sick and tired of buttering up that hard crust on the outside!"

As parents grow gray, the kids are hurling themselves into the daily fray with a joyous zest for combat. I remember the merry gleam in a little girl's eyes when I asked her:

"How do you wake up your brother in the morning?"

"I just open the door and put the cat in his room."

"How does that wake him up?"

"He sleeps with the dog."

Scientists tell us that chickens in a barnyard always form a society based on a "pecking order." At the top is the biggest and strongest chicken, who can peck all the others without ever being pecked back. At the bottom is the hapless fowl who's pecked by everybody. Kids in a large family have a pecking order too, based on age and size, and it's a wise child who knows exactly where he fits in.

One timid little boy whispered to me backstage that if he had his "druthers," he'd be a mouse.

A mouse? Why a mouse? I wondered.

"Because when I ran into my little hole, my brother couldn't follow me."

Here's a story about a boy who was in the fourth grade. Teacher asked him, "Suppose your mother gave you a large apple and a small one, and told you to give one of them to your brother. Which one would you give him?"

"It depends," said the boy cautiously. "Do you mean my big brother or my little brother?"

Middle children such as the lad in that story are usually the bewildered ones. The first-born automatically get attention as the eldest of the brood, and the "babies" receive the loving care that's reserved for the helpless infant. Seven-year-old

Luke expressed the frustration of all kids in the middle when he said:

"My big brother beats me up, and my little sister, Juno, blames me for everything."

"At least your sister has a pretty name," I told him. "Do you know where the name 'Juno' came from?"

"Sure. Juno was the goddess of love—but you'd never guess it from meeting my sister!"

With five little Links of my own, two of them already married and started on families, I'm convinced that big families are the most fun. They're also the best possible place for kids to learn about life. Long before a kid from a large family leaves the nest, he has learned the virtues of getting along with others, and the wisdom of the Golden Rule.

I was an only child. I missed the joys of growing up in a big household, of belonging to a close-knit, loving group. So I felt very close to a certain sad-eyed little girl of six one day when she told me her dearest wish:

"I sure want a brother or a sister, because I'm all alone."

"Have you asked your folks for one?" I inquired.

"Yes, I did. Mommy said 'yes' and Daddy said 'yes' too."

"Well then, I'll just bet you have a new baby at your house one of these days."

She shook her head regretfully. "No," she sighed, "I guess God says 'no.'"

New babies arriving or on their way are a source of endless wonder and excitement among the little ones. Listen to this conversation I had with a four-year-old named Marise:

"I hear you have a new baby around the house."

"Yes, we have a brand new one."
"Do you help your mother with her?"
"I sure do."
"How?"
"I put on the powder."
"What's the most important thing to remember about that?"
"Get it on the right end."

Just as mystified by it all was the nursery schooler in this conversation:

"How many children in your family?"
"There are seven of us."
"That must cost a lot of money."
"Oh, no. We don't buy babies, we raise 'em."

Every big family seems to develop its own set of household rules as life goes along, so that everybody can exist in reasonable harmony. We Linkletters, for example, believe that the family should be together at dinnertime, and not scattered over the house with snacks in front of a tv set. We have an ironclad rule that there's to be no tv-watching or radio-listening, no quarreling or arguments. Dinnertime is a time to pay attention to each other, and we find it's lots of fun.

Some of the family rules that kids tell me about are never intended for the ears of outsiders. There was little Frankie, who said he had five brothers and three sisters, so I asked:

"What are the rules for a family that big?"

"No pushing at the table—and don't go to the bathroom except *in* the bathroom."

Here are some more family rules:

* No screaming, no cussing, no slobbering, no nothing.
* When the sun goes down, the noise goes down.
* Never spit at the dinner table or switch channels during a gun fight.
* Never flush the toilet when someone's in the shower, because the water turns ice cold and you freeze the guy in there.

Remember the story of the little old lady who lived in a shoe and had so many children she didn't know what to do? I thought of her problem when I talked to a youngster from a huge family. I began by asking:

"How many brothers do you have?"

"Ten."

"How many sisters?"

"Four."

"Wow! With fifteen kids in the family, who puts up the biggest howl?"

"Dad does. He has to go next door to shave!"

Here is one of my favorite baby tales about three five-year-olds who were discussing the mystery of how they arrived in this world. "The doctor brought me," said one. "My parents bought me in a store," said the second. And the third said, "My parents were too poor to buy me. I was homemade."

CHAPTER VIII

Be My Valentine

Do you remember your first childhood sweetheart? I had quite a crush on a little girl named Audrey, back in the first grade. She had china blue eyes, long golden curls down her back, and a missing tooth. She was the kind of girl you wanted to hurry up and learn to read and write for, so you could pass notes in class. I planned to elope with her the moment we got to third grade.

I think of Audrey sometimes when I ask the little ones on my show about the romance in their lives. They grin, they giggle, they whoop, they swing their legs and peek out at me from behind their fingers—but they love to confess about their Valentines.

Four-and-a-half-year-old Ellen from nursery school told me what she'd like to do:

"Marry Stevie."

"You mean this nice-looking, red-headed boy sitting next to you?"

"Yes."

I turned to her boy friend, who squirmed in his seat and regarded the girl with something less than adoration.

"What about you, Stevie? Do you want to marry Ellen?"
"No. Never as long as I'm alive!"
"Why not?"

"Every time I turn around at school, she paints my nose."
(There, thought I, was a girl who was making *sure* that her love was a many-splendored thing.)

A generation ago, engaged couples dreamed of honeymooning at Niagara Falls. Today, in the jet age, it's fashionable for young people to plan a wedding trip to Hawaii. But where would the tiny kids like to go if they were being married? Listen to this:

"You're only six years old and you're already planning to get married?"
"Yup."
"Got the girl all picked out?"
"Sure."
"Where are you going for your honeymoon?"
He hesitated a moment, and then told me happily:
"Disneyland!"

Not all boys are broken so easily to the idea of marriage. In fact, the average boy is more apt to despise girls and avoid them like a Saturday night bath—that is, until he's a little older! Now hear this:

"Do you belong to any clubs?"

"Yes, the Women Haters' Club."

"At the age of six? What do you do at the club?"

"We sit around and hate women."

"You mean women like your mothers?"

"Oh, no. Not that kind of women. We hate little girls. We make plans for how to catch them."

"What do you do after you catch them?"

"That's the trouble. We don't know what to do with them."

"You *are* young, aren't you!"

Of all the girls who've ever told me what snips and snails boys can be, I'd say the one who really convinced me was a ten-year-old intellectual who had her mind set on a very unusual career.

"What do you want to be?"

"A herpetologist."

"You're the first girl who ever said that! How come?"

"Because I like snakes better than boys."

"What's so attractive about a snake?"

"They have such beautiful big brown eyes and such sweet faces."

"Then you believe that a boy as a companion definitely comes second to a snake?"

"Oh, no! After a snake comes a lizard, and then a tortoise, then a gila monster, and *then* comes a boy—*maybe!*"

"You're going to make a fine herpetologist!"

High school students imitate adults, kids in junior high imitate the seniors, kids in grammar school imitate the juniors, and so on. Perhaps that's why the current fad of "going steady" has percolated clear down to the eleven-year-olds. They're hardly at the first-date stage, much less ready for a steady, but they're already speculating about it.

Catherine had a practical approach. When I asked what she thought of going steady at the age of eleven, she said:

"I definitely don't believe in it."

"Why not?"

"You can't marry him, so why bother?"

Spoken like a huntress!

❖   ❖   ❖

Jo Ann, you're eleven. What do you think about going steady?

You shouldn't until you're at least thirteen or older. Otherwise it's stupid.

I see. Do you go steady?

Yes.

❖   ❖   ❖

A juvenile prospect for permanent bachelorhood put it this way:
You say you'd like best to live in the Reptile Age. Why?

Because I don't like people or traffic and I could train dinosaurs.
I must point out that there would be no girls, either.
All the better.

❖   ❖   ❖

Here's a young lady who reduces romantic problems to their fundamentals.
Louise, what's your idea of a good husband?
Well, I think he ought to be a man.

❖   ❖   ❖

Here's just the boy with the right outlook for Louise.
What's an ideal wife, Johnny?
Somebody who's a good cook and will tuck you in bed.

❖ ❖ ❖

Six-year-old Steven is catching on in a hurry. I asked him what he'd do if a girl chased him, and he said he'd run.

But if she were pretty, Steve, would you still run?
Yes, but not too fast.

❖ ❖ ❖

Five-year-old Dennis confessed he was so fond of girls that he had two of them. What's more, he planned to marry both of them in June.
But if you do that, you'll be a bigamist.
Sure I'm the bigamist. I'm five. They're just four!

CHAPTER IX

Once Upon a Time

Little children, the very young, are spellbound by stories of fairylands and magic kingdoms, of elves and leprechauns, of unicorns and flying carpets. Their imaginations take wing as they go adventuring with a Peter Pan or a Goldilocks.

It's fun to go along on these imaginary journeys, to let a child take you by the hand and lead you down the enchanted path to storyland. There are so many familiar creatures waiting there to welcome you back to your own childhood—Little Red Riding Hood, Cinderella, the Three Little Pigs, all your old favorites.

I always enjoy these conducted tours of never-never land, but somehow the stories my young guides tell don't sound quite the same as when I was a child.

A girl of five reveals that her favorite story is about Goldilocks. I ask her to tell it, and she does:

"This little girl with gold hair went into this house and there were no bears there, so she ate all their pie."

"Their pie?"

"Yes."

"What does this story teach you?"

"Always take pie along when you go on a picnic."

Another girl saw an entirely different lesson in the adventures of Goldilocks:

"Never get into strange bears' beds!"

A four-year-old boy tells me his favorite story:

"Wittle Wed Widing Hood."

"What did you learn from that story?"

"Not to talk to stwange woofs."

"Little Red Riding Hood" is easily one of the most popular tales. It has everything—a brave little heroine, a kindly old grandma (rest her soul), a villainous old wolf, and a heroic woodsman who dashes to the rescue just in time. And naturally it's the heavy of the drama, the wolf, who gets most of the attention:

"What's the best part of the story, Shirley?"
"When the wolf comes in and climbs into Grandma's birthday suit."

"Jane, how did Little Red Riding Hood find out it was the wolf and not her grandma in bed?"
"She counted the legs. The wolf had four, and her grandma only had two."

"Melissa, how do you think Little Red Riding Hood could tell the difference between a wolf and her grandma?"
"Well, a wolf has a *black* tail."

❖ ❖ ❖

What's your favorite story?
"Cinderella."
What's the lesson there?
Don't buy shoes too big.

❖ ❖ ❖

Do you have a wish?
I want to be a princess.

What does a princess do all day?
  She sits on a gold throne and bosses the prince.
That's what they do, all right!

❖   ❖   ❖

What's your favorite nursery rhyme?
  "Mary had a little lamb, its fleece was white as snow."
What's "fleece"?
  Little bugs.

❖   ❖   ❖

  My favorite is "Humpty Dumpty."
*Why couldn't all the king's horses and all the king's men
put Humpty Dumpty back together again?*
  Because he wasn't hard-boiled.

❖   ❖   ❖

What's your favorite story?
  "Sleeping Beauty."
What do you learn from it?
  It's a good thing to have a prince by your bed.

❖   ❖   ❖

What's your favorite story?
  "The Ugly Duckling."
What does that teach you?
  When you're hatched and you're not pretty enough,
don't cry, because some day maybe you'll turn out to be
Jayne Mansfield.

❖   ❖   ❖

  I like the story of Jack and Jill.
What does it teach you?

Never trust a girl when you're going downhill; they'll always trip you.

❖ ❖ ❖

A nine-year-old boy told me a story in rhyme that I'd never heard before. At least, not quite like this:

"Old Mother Hubbard went to the cupboard, to get her poor daughter a dress. When she got there, the cupboard was bare, and so was her daughter, I guess."

Where did you read a rhyme like that?

In the Cub Scout Manual.

❖ ❖ ❖

If you could be a character in a story, who would you be?

Davy Crockett.

What does his story teach you?

Stay away from the Alamo!

❦ CHAPTER X ❦

Just For Laughs

A JOKE, in this modern age of communications, can travel
around the globe in far less time than it took the first space
man to orbit the earth. I realized this recently when I heard a
brand new political gag ad-libbed in New York just before
I boarded a jet plane for Hollywood. I told my friends the
same joke a few hours later when I reached Hollywood—only
to find that they'd already heard it! Some wag on the long-
distance phone had beaten me to the punch line.

I remembered this incident as I started to put together this
particular chapter, which is a kind of mulligan stew of kid
stories, bright sayings and humorous doings sent in by you
readers and listeners. Duplicates of many of these quips and
stories were sent to me by dozens of different people from
Alabama to Alaska, proving how well traveled humor can be.
This also explains why you may recognize a favorite of your
own in these pages. Personally, I enjoy running across a good
story that I've heard before. It's like meeting a friend.

Just for laughs, let's start our sampler with a few of my
special favorites:

A six-year-old came running in from the back yard and told his father, "Look at this! I pulled this cornstalk up all by myself!"

His father said, "My, you're strong."

"I sure am," the boy replied. "The whole world had hold of the other end."

❖ ❖ ❖

Five-year-old Jeff was trying hard to play his favorite tune on a harmonica that he'd just gotten for his birthday. When a friend asked to hear the tune, he said mournfully, "It's no use. I've played up and down this thing and that song just isn't there."

❖ ❖ ❖

Four-year-old Russ watched as his mother put a fresh diaper on his baby brother. When she neglected to dust the infant with talcum powder, the boy shouted, "Hold it, Mom! You forgot to salt him."

❖ ❖ ❖

A girl at school was very downcast when March 1 came along on the calendar. "I've just learned how to spell February," she explained, "and now it's gone."

❖ ❖ ❖

A boy's description of a muggy day: "It's when everything that's supposed to stick together comes apart, and everything that's supposed to come apart sticks together."

❖ ❖ ❖

A girl in the third grade was having trouble doing her arithmetic without counting on her fingers, so her mother tried to teach her to do sums in her head.

"Close your eyes and imagine you see a blackboard," the mother told her. "Do you see it?"

"Yes," said the girl.

"Now write your problem on it. Do you have it written down?"

"Not yet," the girl said. "I can't find the chalk."

❖ ❖ ❖

A seven-year-old boy was waiting in line at an ice cream stand and hanging on to his three-year-old brother, who kept yelling impatiently, "I want vanilla!" The stand was

out of vanilla, but the older boy handled the situation with all the skill of a child psychologist. He bought two straw-berry cones and handed one to his brother, saying, "Here you are—pink vanilla!"

Any parent knows that children are absolutely ingenious at inventing excuses. The average mother hears more plausible explanations for misdeeds in one week than a traffic judge hears all year. Let's listen to some of these inventive little minds at work:

A boy's mother told him, "You mustn't pull the cat's tail like that."

"I'm only holding it, Mom," he said. "The cat is pulling."

❖ ❖ ❖

Asked why he always gobbled his food, a nine-year-old explained:

"It tastes so good that I want to eat all I can before I lose my appetite."

❖ ❖ ❖

A mother asked her daughter, "Why can't you behave like Sally next door?"

"Because she's a doctor's kid," the girl said.

"What's that got to do with it?" her mother demanded.

"The doctor always keeps the best babies for himself," the girl replied.

❖ ❖ ❖

One of the funniest sketches I've ever heard is comedian Shelley Berman making a telephone call that is answered by a very small child. If you've ever had the experience of dialing a friend and getting one of his little kids instead, you know how hilariously frustrating it can be. Here are a few "telephone" stories:

A five-year-old boy answered a phone call from a salesman and told him that his mother wasn't home.

"Is there anybody else there that I can talk to?" the salesman asked.

"My sister," the boy replied.

Several minutes went by while the salesman waited patiently. At last the boy came back on the line and said, "I'm sorry, mister, but I can't lift her out of the play-pen."

❖ ❖ ❖

A little girl was very businesslike when she answered the telephone for a caller:

"I'm very sorry," she said, "but my mother has gone to the store. Do you want to leave a message?"

"Yes," said the caller. "Tell her Mr. Whitney called about the television set."

"Okay," said the girl. "How do you spell Whitney?"

"W-H-I-T-N-E-Y."

"Okay. How do you make a 'W'?"

❖ ❖ ❖

A man and his wife were hanging pictures in their new home, and the wife suggested that they "stagger" the pictures up the stairway wall for a smarter effect. Just then the phone rang, and their six-year-old son answered, telling the caller:

"Neither my mom or dad can come right now. My

father is staggering up the stairs and my mother is helping him."

The battle between the sexes seems to begin as soon as the combatants discover which side they're on. I heard this story about one eight-year-old girl talking to a seven-year-old whom she had a crush on. "Come on," she urged him, "let's kiss. You press against me with your lips, and I'll press against you with my lips."

"Okay," said the boy warily. "And the one who presses the hardest wins."

❖ ❖ ❖

Another girl, a first grader named Jeanne, informed her mother that she had broken her engagement to a classmate. "What's the matter?" her mother asked.

"He just isn't ready for marriage yet," the girl explained. "Besides," she added, "he scribbled in my coloring book."

❖ ❖ ❖

A four-year-old had gotten a bad sunburn and it was beginning to flake off. One day his mother heard him muttering to himself as he washed his face: "Only four years old —and wearing out already."

The subject of babies and where they come from is as fascinating as ever to kids, although the modern youngsters do seem more sophisticated about it. The other day I heard of a father who complained that he'd done his best to explain to his son about the birds and the bees—but the boy kept switching the conversation back to girls!

Another boy cornered his reluctant dad one day and said, "Dad, where did I come from?" Father mopped his brow and decided he couldn't evade the question any longer, so he told all while the boy squirmed and fidgeted. When it was over, Dad sighed with relief and said, "Tell me, son, what made you decide to ask me where you came from?" The boy said, "Well, the new kid across the street says *he* comes from Ohio—and I wanted to know where *I* came from."

❖ ❖ ❖

A five-year-old came home from a birthday party and told his modern mother, "I'm never going to believe another word you say. I was the only kid at the party who didn't know that babies are brought by the stork."

❖ ❖ ❖

A mother had just brought her newborn triplets home from the hospital. Her older boy, a five-year-old, took his first doubtful look at the new babies and said, "We'd better start calling folks. They're going to be a lot harder to get rid of than kittens."

❖ ❖ ❖

A boy asked his mother, "Why can't we have a baby?"
"They cost too much," said his mother.
"How much do they cost?" he persisted.
"About three hundred dollars," she said.
"Oh," said the boy. "That's not much, considering how long they last!"

❖ ❖ ❖

A six-year-old boy was utterly fascinated by the hairless condition of his newborn brother.
"Where did you say we got him?" he asked his mother.
"From heaven," she said.
"Boy," he said, "they sure do give 'em close haircuts in heaven."

❖ ❖ ❖

A seven-year-old from a large family was told by the nurse that the stork had left him another baby sister. The nurse asked whether he'd like to see her.

"I've seen lots of babies, so I don't care," the boy said. "But if it's okay, I'd sure like to see that stork!"

❖ ❖ ❖

I can sympathize with this boy who called the dentist's office and said, "I'm supposed to make an appointment."

"I'm sorry," said the nurse, "but the dentist is out of town."

"Thank you," said the boy. "When will he be out of town again?"

❖ ❖ ❖

Another youngster was getting his third polio shot and the doctor asked which arm he'd like it in.

The boy had an instant reply:

"Mother's!"

❖ ❖ ❖

A boy's uncle was surprised to find him home and told him, "I thought you were in school. Are you all right?"

"I'm fine," said the boy. "I'm sick."

❖ ❖ ❖

An eight-year-old girl asked her neighbors if she could baby-sit for them. When they asked what she'd charge, she submitted this list of prices: "Sleeping babies, 25¢; Crying babies, 35¢; Wet babies, 40¢; Worse than wet babies, 50¢."

❖ ❖ ❖

A mother asked her son why he didn't take his little sister along as he left to go fishing, and he said, "Because the last time I took her I didn't catch a thing."

Mother said, "I'm sure she'll be quiet if you explain to her."

"Oh, it wasn't the noise," the boy replied. "She ate the bait."

❖   ❖   ❖

A man woke early one morning and decided to surprise the family by making oatmeal for everybody for breakfast. He was spooning out a bowl for his four-year-old son Freddie when the boy walked into the kitchen.

"Want honey on it?" the father asked.

"Yes," said Freddie.

"And milk?"

"Yes."

"Butter, too?"

"Yes."

He gave the bowl to the boy. Freddie just stared at it and then pushed it away.

"What's the matter?" his dad asked. "I put everything you wanted on it."

Freddie answered, "I don't like oatmeal."

Maybe it's because my father was an evangelist, but I have a special fondness for stories about Sunday School and church folk in general. Here are some favorites of mine:

A kindergarten-age Sunday School class was expecting a visit from the minister the following week, so the teacher was carefully rehearsing the kids for the big event. Little Jimmy was told that when the minister asked somebody to tell who made him, he was to stand up and say, "God made me, Reverend," while the others remained very quiet.

The visit day arrived and everything went perfectly until the pastor asked the question: "Can anybody tell me who made us?"

There was an uneasy silence, so he repeated the question. Nobody answered.

Finally a little girl raised her hand and explained: "The boy that God made is home sick with the measles."

❖ ❖ ❖

Asked by his mother what he'd learned in Sunday School, ten-year-old Bobby launched into an exciting tale:

"Teacher told us about when God sent Moses behind the enemy lines to rescue the Israelites from the Egyptians. When they came to the Red Sea, Moses called for the engineers to build a pontoon bridge. And after they'd all crossed, they looked back and saw the Egyptian tanks coming. Moses radioed headquarters on his walkie-talkie to send bombers to blow up the bridge, and that saved the Israelites."

"Bobby!" said his mother. "Is that really the way your teacher told you that story?"

"Well, not exactly," the boy admitted. "But if I told it *her* way, you'd never believe it!"

❖ ❖ ❖

Taken to church for the first time, a four-year-old girl was quite impressed. As everyone knelt down, she whispered, "Mommy, what are they doing now?"

"Shhhh," said her mother. "They're getting ready to say their prayers."

"What?" yelled the astonished child. "With all their clothes on?"

❖ ❖ ❖

A family invited their minister and his wife to dinner. After the good man had said grace, the family's little boy looked at him and said, "Gosh, you don't pray near as long when you're ready for dinner, do you?"

❖ ❖ ❖

A woman with a reputation for a sharp tongue was telling her neighbor about the weekly church service. She
complained that the seats had been hard, the choir was off-
key and the preaching was uninspiring. Just then, her
daughter, who'd been with her as the collection plate came
by, said: "But Mama, what can you expect for a dime?"

❖ ❖ ❖

One of my listeners up in Alaska, Mrs. Josephine Seltzer,
wrote me about the time that she tried to find out which of
her boys had misbehaved. As she put them to bed, she told
them, "I'm going into my room and say my prayers, and
I'll ask God to let me know which one of you was bad
today. Wouldn't you like to tell me *before* I ask God?"

One of the boys answered promptly: "No, Mommy,
we'll just wait and see what God has to say."

Now let's sample a few stories about schools, teachers and
pupils. I loved the boy's reply when his dad asked if he had
been a good boy at school that day. "I sure was," the boy
said. "You can't get into much trouble when you're standing
in the corner all day."

❖ ❖ ❖

A seven-year-old told his teacher, "I don't want to scare
you, but my daddy says that if I don't get better grades,
somebody's going to get spanked."

❖ ❖ ❖

A six-year-old boy was curious about the ballot boxes that
were set up in the school gymnasium for an election. Told

by a school official that the boxes were for voting, the boy said, "That's swell! I'm sure glad they're going to elect some new teachers."

❖   ❖   ❖

A teacher asked seven-year-old Johnny whether George Washington had been a soldier or a sailor before he became President. "A soldier," said the boy. Asked how he knew, he said, "I've seen a picture of him crossing the Delaware River, and no *sailor* would stand up in a boat like that."

❖ ❖ ❖

The grammar school class was studying the alphabet. "What comes after T?" the teacher asked. A little girl quickly answered: "V."

❖ ❖ ❖

A group of boys were on their way to the movies to see a cowboy picture, but one objected to it because he'd heard it had too many kissing scenes. One of his pals said, "That's okay—when the kissing starts, we can close our eyes and pretend he's choking her."

❖ ❖ ❖

A five-year-old boy rushed home from kindergarten and begged his mother to buy him a pair of six-shooters. His mother said, "What for? Don't tell me you need those guns for school."

"I sure do," the boy said. "Teacher said that tomorrow she's going to teach us how to draw."

❖ ❖ ❖

A woman ran out of Christmas cards at the last minute, so she sent her ten-year-old daughter out to buy a dozen cards. The girl returned with a box of twelve identical cards. After hastily mailing seven of the cards, the mother happened to read the verse on one that was left. It said: "This little card is just to say, a gift you'll love is on the way."

CHAPTER XI

Nursery Nuggets

THERE's a story that's told of a four-year-old boy who was visiting a farm for the first time and was taken to see the lambs. Finally he worked up enough courage to pat one. "Why," he said delightedly, "they make them out of blankets!"

Lambs are made of blankets, people live in pumpkins, and cows really do jump over the moon in the fanciful imaginings of nursery-schoolers. Happily, they haven't been weaned yet from the fantasy that nourishes their minds. They have no idea where the magic of pretending leaves off and realities begin.

Let's take a trip now, back through time, back through the years since we were four-year-olds, and see what dreams we've left trailing behind.

A little girl with dark blond curls and a blue ribbon in her hair looks very much in earnest as she tells me what she wants to do with her life:

"I want to be a nurse and fix up sick people."

"What would you do if I came into your office with a broken arm, a broken leg and a broken neck?"

"I'd cry."

A nursery babe smiles up at me. "How did your folks meet?" I ask her.

"It happened in heaven."

"How?"

"They were babies waiting to be born, and God put them on the same cloud."

What is it like to be four? It's to be like the boy who brought his puppy to visit his grandmother. She was busy fixing dinner and paid no attention to the pup. After a while the boy, his eyes filling with tears, asked her reproachfully: "Aren't you even going to speak to your granddog?"

Another tiny moppet is waiting to be vaccinated, but she's determined to be brave. All goes well until she is face to face with the needle. Now she leans over and speaks softly into the doctor's ear: "I think your mother is calling you."

Few things in childhood have the delicious excitement of a genuine secret. The trouble with secrets is they bubble up inside a child until they just have to bubble out.

❖   ❖   ❖

What's your favorite game?
   Hide-and-seek.
Why?
   Because no one can ever find me.
Where do you hide?

   I can't tell; it's a secret.
Come on, you can tell me, and I'll never tell anybody.
   All right. It's in the garbage can.

❖   ❖   ❖

What do you do for fun?
   I play dog.
Who do you play it with?

My dog.
How do you play dog with a dog?
  I bite his tail, and he bites mine!"

❖ ❖ ❖

What's best about nursery school, Frank?
  Making castles in the sand pile.

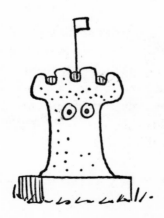

What's the hardest thing you have to do at the nursery?
Get the sand out of my pants before I go home.

❖   ❖   ❖

What do you like best in kindergarten?
Hot Scotch.

Most of the children I've encountered are warm, outgoing, responsive and merry of heart. As I look at them each day, I sometimes wonder what it is about growing up that changes these charming creatures into workaday, lackluster, predictable adults. It must be the many frustrations, disappointments, worries and tensions that life brings that grind the bright facets of a child down to the flat grays of adulthood. All the more reason for us, then, to enjoy the sparkle of a child like five-year-old Scotty.

"You look a little the worse for wear, Scotty. What gave you that bruise on your face?"

Scotty shrugged. "It's nothing much. I was just sitting at the bar at our house and I fell off the stool."

"What do you do when you're not hanging around the bar at home?"

"I work a lot of puzzles at nursery school. They're easy."

"What's the hardest thing about nursery school?"

"Unbuttoning my pants. Want me to show you?"

"No! I believe you. You're a pretty smart boy, Scotty. Can you tell your right hand from your left hand?"

"Sure—my right is the north one, and my left is the west."

"What do you think of the saying, 'The early bird gets the worm?' "

"He's welcome to it. I ate one once and it tasted like cold spaghetti."

"What would you do if you could be invisible for a day?"
I asked some five-year-olds, and here's what they told me:

❖ I'd change all the clocks to different times and mix everybody up.

❖ I'd rob a bank and buy a toy store.

❖ I'd marry some nice fellow before he knew what was
happening.

❖ I'd take a big bottle of hair remover and go around remov-
ing everybody's hair. I'd do it at night, and in the morning
they'd all wake up bald. Wouldn't that be fun?
It sure would!

During lunch at the Brown Derby not long ago, I was
talking to one of my favorite comedians, Alan Young. He was
bemoaning the lack of material available, and the relative
scarcity of creative comedy writers. Then he turned to me
with a thoughtful, envious look and said: "You're really
lucky, Art. Those kids you talk to are the greatest natural
comedians there are. You'll never run out of material!" And
he's right.

Sometimes I have the feeling that some of the kids *do* have
writers, like four-year-old Stephen. I asked him:

"Do you know what a weasel is?"

"Sure," he said. "Weasels are things that break out all over
your face."

"Who would you rather have spank you—Mom or Dad?"

"Mommy, always."

"Where does she spank you?"

"In my room."

What do you want to be, Mary Lou?
   A cowboy girl.
What does a cowboy girl do?
   She fights Indians and milks cows.
How do you milk a cow?
   I don't know, but it has something to do with those hoses on its fanny.

Three-year-old Steve was one of the brightest of the tiny youngsters we've ever had on the show, but his notions on the operations of a modern dairy were delightfully mixed up. After revealing that his parents had taken him on a dairy tour, he gave this version of the expedition:

"There's this big brown cow with the red eyes and wet tongue, and he has a balloon under him full of nipples. The man gets a pail of milk and a fire hose, and they put the fire hose on one of the nipples, and put the other end in the milk pail—and then they turn on this machine and fill the cow full of milk!"

Like Sir Lancelot in "Camelot," six-year-old Timothy assured me that he was perfect in every way.
   "Don't you have *any* bad habits?" I persisted.
   "Maybe one," he admitted. "I drink—out of the bathtub."

Being small has its own special hazards, as I realized when I talked to little Keith about his vacation.
   "Did you have fun?" I asked.
   "Yes, but nothing much happened."
   "Didn't *anything* happen at all?
   "Well, a rooster bit me on the belly button."

To the very young, any knowledge whatever is a source of great pride. For example:

"Can you tell your right from your left?"

"No."

"Well, then, what *do* you know?"

"I know my front from my back."

❖ ❖ ❖

What's the funniest thing that happened to you, Linda?

My mom told me to go lay an egg.

What's so funny about that?

I don't know how.

❖ ❖ ❖

You don't look very happy today, George. What's your problem?

I met a big dog on my way to the studio, and he tore the zipper right off my pants.

❖ ❖ ❖

How do you help your mother with the new baby, Hazel?
I fold diapers and put the powder in the seat—but it's hopeless.
What do you mean, "it's hopeless"?
Diapers on *that* baby never last longer than five minutes.

On gray days when my spirits tend to droop, and I'm tempted to wonder if my television efforts are worth the doing, I can console myself with the thought that if nothing else, my "House Party" visits with the kids insure that every Monday through Friday in the U.S.A., four small children are thoroughly and completely scrubbed. Necks and ears and elbows fairly gleam with the exertions of proud mothers who are determined that their progeny shall really be clean for this once in their lives.

Four-year-old Michele was glowing and rosy-cheeked with cleanliness, so I complimented her:

"You look like something just off the top of a birthday cake. How'd you get so pretty?"

"My mommy washed and washed me this morning while I stood on the toilet."

One of the most perplexing problems of the very young is to figure out their relationships with aunts, uncles, cousins and grandparents. Just for fun, I asked a group of nursery schoolers what a grandmother was. To my surprise, they all had a fairly good idea of grandma's doings:

❖ A grandmother is the nice old lady who comes to visit you, and you have to clean up the house before she gets there.

❖ She's somebody who cooks good spaghetti dinners.

❖ She's the baby sitter who does it for nothing.
   (*We grandfathers get the same wages!*)

Pretending can be very real to a child. I like the story of Cindy, who wanted to be a doctor when she grew up. Mostly she bandaged and cared for her dolls, but once in a while she'd go on an imaginary sick call to someone in the neighborhood. One day she ran out on such a mercy errand, forgetting to close the door behind her. When her mother insisted she come back and shut it, the girl did so and raced away. Later on, Cindy's mother asked how the patient was getting along. "She died," Cindy said. "Died while I was closing that darn door."

Many girls want to be nurses, like five-year-old Nancy. I asked her, "What's the hardest thing a nurse has to do?"

"Take care of fussy patients."

"How would you calm them down if they were fussy?" I asked.

"Kiss 'em," she said.

Michael, age five, said he wanted to be a specialist.

"Do you know what a specialist does?"

"Sure. He takes care of special people like George Washington and Marilyn Monroe."

"If you were going to take a trip to the moon and you only had one suitcase, what would you pack?"

❖ (Barbara, 3) My doll and my mommy and daddy.

❖ (Vicki, 3½) I don't want to go to the moon.

❖ (Danny, 3) The bathroom.

❖ (Steve, 4) Spaghetti.

❖ ❖ ❖

What do you want to be, Margie?
  A mother. The kind that has babies.

❖ ❖ ❖

What's your ambition?
  To be a skin diver in the Navy.
What if you saw a man-eating shark?
  I'd tell him, "Go find a man; I'm just a little boy."

❖ ❖ ❖

What will you be some day, Sharon?
  A movie star.
I'll give you an acting job: Say "Arthur!" like you're angry.
  "Arthur! Like you're angry!"

❖ ❖ ❖

What do you want to be, Donald?
  An artist so I can draw rainbows.
What's at the end of the rainbow?
  A plug.
Where have you been seeing your rainbows?
  In the bathtub.

❖ ❖ ❖

What do you want to be?
  A policeman.
What's the most important thing to remember?
  Don't wet your bed.

❖ ❖ ❖

What's your ambition?

To be a fireman.

What if you saw a big fat lady in a tall building yelling for help?

I'd send her a big fat fireman.

CHAPTER XII

Jet Pilots and Ballerinas

CHILDREN are forever daydreaming about the glamorous and exciting jobs they'll have when they grow up. What's often surprising is to see how early these ambitions seem to develop. By the time a boy is three, he is already picturing himself as somebody big and important, like the corner policeman with his badge and whistle. Little sister is already being a good mother to her dolls, kissing them when they're good and spanking them when they're naughty.

Through the years, I've had dozens of future doctors and nurses gravely examine me and prescribe all sorts of remarkable remedies for my imaginary ailments. They've assured me that aspirin will fix a broken neck, and that the hole in my head won't bother me if I put a cork in it. Incidentally, I've learned along the way that the favorite treatment of all young medics for their patients is a shot administered in the likeliest spot. Shots are prescribed for any and everything, and always with a certain eagerness that betrays the child-doctor's heartfelt desire to see someone else get the needle for a change.

I've gone soaring through imaginary skies with fledgling jet pilots at the controls, gone swimming while a confident five-year-old lifeguard kept watch, and had fun sliding down the station house pole with six-year-old firemen.

Little ballerinas have danced through my mind, and future Sarah Bernhardts have been my leading ladies in scenes that I'll always remember.

A typical group of six-year-olds sits before me, including a future major league ballplayer, a nurse, a fireman and a dressmaker. I ask the ballplayer:

"What position do you want to play?"
"Pitcher."

"What's the most important step in becoming a great pitcher?"
"Making friends with the umpire."

❖   ❖   ❖

The nurse tells me the hardest part of her job:
"Being nice to all the cranky patients."
"What's the most fun for a nurse?" I ask her.

Her smile is pure joy as she tells me:

"Giving them shots when they're not looking."

❖   ❖   ❖

Now I move on to the girl who wants to be a dressmaker like her mother, and ask her:

"What's the hardest thing about that job?"

"After you've been working on a dress," she tells me,
"you hope it fits in the end."

Some children are natural spotlight seekers who revel in
the idea that my studio audience is enjoying their remarks.
But once in a while there's a child who is warier and less
outgoing, and is in need of friendly reassurance.

The warning signal for me is flashed in a child's eyes when
the audience laughs at what he considers to be a perfectly
sensible remark. For example, I ask a seven-year-old what he
wouldn't want to be when he grows up, and he says: "A
garbage man. I think it's a stinking job." The solid wave of
laughter washes across the stage and hits him with telling im-
pact. He was completely unaware of the double nature of his
answer, and he's ready to retreat into silence or one-syllable
answers unless I'm on his side with a friendly word, or an
explanation that he is a very funny young man.

If I think the alarm is a serious one, my next question will
always be something harmless, such as, "Do you have any
brothers or sisters?" Even then I can be fooled when an answer
comes back: "No, but Mommy says we'll get some the minute Daddy gets rested up." Once again the laughter hits the
stage, and reassurances are called for.

And so, with a fond pat on the head, I move on to the next
child, returning only after all is well and we've changed the
subject completely.

There was a time when all young boys wanted to be rail-road engineers. Now the most glamorous job seems to be a jet pilot. One future pilot told me he'd like to fly clear around the world, so I asked him:

What would you do if you lost your way over the mountains?

I'd ask my mama because she never gets herself losted.

❖   ❖   ❖

What would you do if you ran out of gas over the Pacific?

Tell the passengers to fasten their safety belts.

Then what?

I'd bail out!

When the laugh subsided, he explained in a tone of hurt dignity:

I'd come back! I was just going to get gas!

Being the tiny, helpless creatures that they are, all kids yearn for the day when *they* will have the power to tell everybody else what to do. Wistfully they eye that perfect symbol of heroic authority, the smartly uniformed policeman. I can only hope that some of the kids I've talked to really do become officers, because I like their novel ideas about law enforcement.

"Stephen, why do you want to be a police officer?"

"So I could ride a motorcycle and stop pretty girls."

"What kind of tickets would you give them?"

"Oh," he protested, "you don't give *them* tickets. You just stop and talk to them."

(We've all seen those dashing young patrolmen do just that!)

The problem that bedevils all these potential officers of the law is how to recognize a bad man who ought to be arrested. One boy led me in a complete circle of confusion, when I asked:

"What does a bad man look like?"

"Like a robber."

"What does a robber look like?"

"A burglar."

"What does a burglar look like?"

"A bad man."

There we were, back where we started!

Two other officers had sure-fire ways of recognizing bad men:

* You can tell they're bad because they wear black and white striped uniforms.

* You know they're bad because people boo and hiss them!

When I was a boy, I was convinced that the most glamorous and exciting job in the world was a fireman. What a thrill it was to see a hook-and-ladder truck come roaring down the street, with its siren wailing and its lights winking red! I could just picture my heroes as they reached the blaze, plunging fearlessly through the smoke and carrying unconscious damsels to safety. I can still feel the tug of that early ambition when I meet a young smoke eater.

"So you want to be a fireman. What's the hardest thing a fireman does?"

"Puts out fires."

"That's right. What's the easiest thing a fireman does?"

"Plays poker all day at the station."

"How do you know that?"

"My dad's a fireman."

Another six-year-old had a different idea of the fire fighter's life. I asked him:

"What's the hardest thing a fireman does?"

"When you get out of bed for a fire, be sure not to put your pants on backwards."

Kids seem to be sharply divided over the whole idea of whether they'd enter the medical profession. Some like to picture themselves at the patient's bedside, being reassuring and helpful as their own family doctors are. But other youngsters think about the perils of the operating room, and have no desire to tinker with the insides of their fellow men.

What do you want to be?
  A doctor.
Why?
  My mom has lots of doctor bills, and if I was a doctor I'd only charge her two cents to take anything out.

❖   ❖   ❖

What do you want to be?
  A pediatrician.
What's the hardest part of that job?
  Putting kids back together again.

Along with the fun and laughter about jobs and professions, there are times when a very serious youngster will convince me that he is already dedicated to a calling. Such a boy made us all stop and think one day when he revealed that he wanted to be a neurologist like his dad.

"Why do you want to be a neurologist?" I asked.

"Because when I grow up, if the world is still here, I think people will be more nervous than they are today."

The call of the Wild West is as strong as ever in the hearts of the young.

"I want to be a cowboy," said six-year-old Bobby.

"Why?"

"Because I see them all the time on tv and they never take baths."

"What do you want to be?"

"A cowboy."

"Do you know how to milk a cow?"

"Sure. You just pull its faucets."

❖   ❖   ❖

What would you be?
  A beatnik.
Can you talk in "beatnik"?
  Sure.

Give us some beatnik talk.
  Like that's swinging, man!
What does that mean?
  I don't know.

If all childhood ambitions actually came true, we'd have more nurses in our hospitals than patients. Nursing has a runaway popularity among little girls, with its combined appeal of pretty uniforms and the chance to "mother" the patients.

What do you want to be, Emily?
   A nurse so I can help sick people get better.
What's the first thing a nurse says to a patient when he walks into the office?
   Hello, lay down, relax; I'm going to give you a shot.

❖   ❖   ❖

What do you want to be?
   A nurse.
What's the most important thing to remember?
   To smile and tell everybody they have to wait an hour.

❖   ❖   ❖

So you want to be a nurse. What if I came in with a stomach ache?
   I'd give you a shot.
What if I had smallpox?
   I'd give you a shot.
What if I had chickenpox?
   Another shot.
What if I just had a runny nose?
   I'd wipe it.

❖   ❖   ❖

What would you like to be?
   A ballerina with a fluffy skirt.
What's the hardest thing a ballerina does?
   Zip up the back of her dress.

❖   ❖   ❖

What's your ambition?
   To be Miss Universe.
How do you get to be that?
   You grow up and have everything in the right place.

❖   ❖   ❖

Karen, what would you like to be?

   A dog.
Why?
   I love to lick people.

❖   ❖   ❖

What's your ambition?
   To be a cowgirl.
What's the first thing to do when you milk a cow?
   Get a bottle.

❖   ❖   ❖

What do you want to be?
   A mother with three children.

What kind of husband do you want?
I don't want one.

"What do you want to be?"
"An actress."
"All right, let's act out a scene together: Will you marry me and drive away into the sunset in my big, beautiful new car?"
"No. I get car sick."

"What do you want to be?"
"A football player."
"What position?"
"Third base."

Seven-year-old Noel wanted to be a pianist.
"What's the most important thing a pianist must remember?"
"To wash his hands before he sits down to play."

Here's a semi-sophisticated eleven-year-old:
"What do you want to be?"
"A writer."

"Give me an example of what you'd write."

"Okay. It's called, What America Means Today, and it's the story of a tree. The trunk is the Government, the limbs are the States, and the leaves are the people. The green leaves are good people, and the brown leaves are bad people."

"What about our national leaders? Where are they?"

"Kennedy is the roots—and Nixon's out on a limb!"

Ten-year-old Sheryl had one of the most unusual ambitions for a girl that I've ever heard.

"I want to be a television producer and star in my own show," she said.

"What would you call it?"

"Opposites."

"How would it work?"

"Everybody would do opposite things. I'd have Red Skelton sing, Garry Moore would do opera, and you would dance."

(Sounds like an interesting show, doesn't it? Guess I'd better get started on my dancing lessons. I figure she won't be on the air for another ten years or so, but I'll need all the practice I can get!)

I never cease to be amazed that in this land of liberty, where every boy can grow up to be President, almost none of them wants to be.

Would you like to be President?
    Not me!

Why not?

Because no matter what happens, it's all your fault!

(I can just hear a succession of Presidents, from George Washington to the present day, saying "Amen!")

❖ ❖ ❖

Although kids stand in awe of the Presidency, they generally think they can handle the Vice President's job with no trouble at all.

Would you like to be President?

Nope. I'm just normal and you have to be better to be President.

How about the Vice President?

Okay, I'll be that.

❖ ❖ ❖

What do you want to be?

Either a waiter or the Vice President.

There's a strange choice. Why those two?

I've had experience as a waiter, and besides, I inherited knowing how from my mother. She's a waitress.

How about being the Vice President?

It sounds like a fun job.

Why not be President?

Oh, I'm not that smart!

❖ ❖ ❖

There was more truth than comedy in the words of one young man who wanted to be a general in our Air Force.

I asked him what's the most important thing an Air Force general has to do, and he told me:

"Be sure you are fighting the right war."

❖ ❖ ❖

What do you want to be?
    A lifeguard.
Suppose you saw a man drowning. What would you do first?
    Build a raft.

❖ ❖ ❖

What do you want to be?
    A mailman.
What's the hardest thing about the mailman's job?
    Climbing the big hill in front of our house.
What does the mailman do for fun?
    He kisses the lady next door.
I guess he just loves playing post office!

❖ ❖ ❖

What do you hope to be?
An engineer on the train from California to Las Vegas.
Why is Las Vegas famous?
Because my mom and dad got married there.
When was that?
Last month.

❖ ❖ ❖

What do you want to be?
A woodchopper, because I love to see those great big trees come falling down in the forest.
What do you yell when a big tree starts to fall?
Help!

❧ CHAPTER XIII ❧

Tales Out of School

Down in Mississippi, there's a grammar school teacher who has worked out a clever way to deal with mothers and fathers. Each semester she pins a note on the jackets of the kids entering her class, saying:

"Dear Parents: If you'll promise not to believe everything your child tells you that happens in school, I'll promise not to believe everything I hear about what happens at home."

After hearing the tall tales that kids spin about *both* parents and teachers, that sounds like a fair exchange to me!

The Very Important Person around any school is the principal. He is expected to be a pillar of dignity, as the symbol of The School to The Community. I could just picture one principal's starched collar wilting on him the day that a seven-year-old girl gave me this version of his high office:

"Our principal's main job is to keep all the mothers happy."

"How does he do that?"

"I don't know," she said. "He always shuts his office door when they go in there."

The average schoolteacher is a heroine in my book, and come to think of it, this *is* my book. All day she battles a tidal

124

surge of high-spirited kids swirling in and out of her classroom. And then, when the last bell rings and they all go whooping off for home, she remains behind to grade papers or go to faculty meetings. Bless those teachers, I say, for sticking to a job year after year that is traditionally overworked and underpaid, and for doing it with such dedicated determination.

Of course, teachers are as human as the rest of us. They can be just as grateful when a school day ends as a mother is when it begins. And sometimes I suspect that a teacher has sent me her four holiest terrors.

A little boy who's been a handful ever since he reached the studio sits there kicking and fidgeting as I ask him:

"Why were you picked to come here today."

"I'm not sure," he says. "But I think teacher wanted to get rid of me for a day."

❖ ❖ ❖

A five-year-old put his teacher squarely on the hot seat when he told why his teacher had sent him:

"Because my mother *doesn't* belong to the PTA."

❖ ❖ ❖

More often than not, it's the child whose mother *does* belong to the PTA who gets teacher's nod. One ten-year-old boy knew he just couldn't miss being selected, and he told me why:

"My mother's president of the PTA, and my favorite teacher was just chosen principal."

That's the way the world goes—it helps to have connections.

❖ ❖ ❖

Why were you chosen to come to the show?

You want to know the honest truth?
Yes.
Because I'm a blabbermouth.
Who says so?
My teacher.

❖   ❖   ❖

Why were you chosen?
Mom makes punch for the teachers' parties.
Is she the best punch maker in the whole school?
I don't think so, because I drank some and I was awful sick all night.

Children look up to their teachers with much of the same mingled love and respect that they feel for their parents. So it's not surprising that many of the young ones want to teach when they grow up. Their reasons for this ambition, however, can be a little disconcerting.

❖   ❖   ❖

What do you want to be?
A teacher.
What's the most important thing for a teacher to remember?
Don't be soft-hearted.

❖   ❖   ❖

Occasionally I meet a child who sees the teacher's side of the daily strife.

What do you want to teach?
Kindergarten.
Why kindergarten?
Because I am in the second grade, and we are pretty terrible already!

❖   ❖   ❖

Why do you want to be a teacher?
Because I'd make such a good one.
What makes you think so?
I'm a born squealer.

IT TAKES ONE TO KNOW ONE!

Four seven-year-olds told me their ideas on what a perfect schoolteacher would be like:

❖ A man who looks like Rock Hudson, sings like Frankie Avalon, gives no homework and is easy with grades.

❖ A lady who looks like Marilyn Monroe.

❖ Somebody who doesn't punish us unless it's absolutely, positively necessary, like if you've just broken the window in the principal's office and not like you fudged into the lunch-line in front of somebody.

❖ Somebody like my teacher, Mrs. Tighe, who gave me all A's and all Excellents—and she's sitting right down there in the front row!

Do you prefer men or women teachers?
Men.
Why?
Because they're more reasonable. Women wait and wait until finally they get even with you.

❖ ❖ ❖

Portia, how would an eleven-year-old like you change school?
We're living in an instant age, you know, like we have instant coffee, tea, soup and potatoes. So I would condense all the classes and all the homework so we could have instant education.

❖ ❖ ❖

What subject would you like to skip in school?
Anatomy.
Do you know what anatomy is?
It's some kind of advanced arithmetic. You don't learn it until you get to college.
Come to think of it, you do learn a little about it in college.

❖ ❖ ❖

What have you done that was interesting in school lately?
I ran for Student Body President, and my slogan was,

"A thinking man's candidate—a voting man's choice."
What happened?
I lost.

❖ ❖ ❖

I asked a panel of first graders to name their best subjects in school. Here they are:

❖ Tether Ball.

❖ Four Square Bean Bag.

❖ Recess.

❖ Bingo.

❖ ❖ ❖

Another group of candid youngsters revealed how coming to the "House Party" show had changed the course of their lives:

❖ I took my first bath in a long time.

❖ My sister's been nice to me for the first time in her life.

❖ I got my first real haircut from a real barber.

❖ I've been giving autographs to everybody.

❖ ❖ ❖

What's the best part of school?
   Lunch.
What's the worst part?
   Writing.
Why is writing so hard?
   I can't read.

❖ ❖ ❖

What do you think of school?
   It's swell, but not arithmetic.
What's the best part?
   Walking home.

❖ ❖ ❖

What do you like best at school?
   Playing baseball.
What position?
   At bat.

What's the most important thing to remember?
If you miss the ball, don't wrap the bat around your neck.

Kids love slang, and there's a new language constantly being created under our very ears. Here are some of the newest expressions around school:

❖ Chicken and skins.
  (A gal with furs.)

❖ Whipped with an ugly stick.
  (Ruined.)

❖ Skitchiest.
  (Some one smart, or hip.)

❖ Pull up the shades.
  (Open your eyes.)

❖ Let's make Z's.
  (Go to sleep.)

❖ Sling me a ring.
  (Marry me.)

Just for good measure, here's a thought for the day, straight from the playground philosophers:
"Never stick your head in the washing machine; you may get a sock in the face."

If you look around the attic among your old treasures and keepsakes, chances are you'll find an old faded class annual or autograph book with the signatures of your schoolmates in it. Remember how we used to rush around at the end of a semester, having all our friends sign up and write silly poems in our books? Kids are still doing it today—and whenever I'm asked for an autograph, my price is a peek in their books.

Here are some of the verses going around the schoolyards these days:

❖ Roses are red, violets are black,
   You look best with a knife in the back.

❖ Roses are red, violets are blue,
   You've got a nose like a B-52.

❖ I saw you in the ocean,
   I saw you in the sea.
   I saw you in the bathtub—
   Oops! Pardon me!

❖ God made butter, God made cheese,
   God made Janet for Jeffrey to squeeze.

❖ Roses are red, violets are blue,
   I know because I saw them hanging on the line.

❖ It's hard to lose a guy when your heart's full of hope,
   But its worse to lose a towel when your eyes are full of soap.

❖ Don't make love near the garden gate,
   'Cause love is blind but the neighbors ain't.

CHAPTER XIV

Little People Are Funny

Picture an Air Force radar station, with its huge antenna endlessly revolving as it scans the skies, gathering a marvelously detailed and continuously changing picture of everything within its vast range.

But seated at the controls is an earnest new recruit who hasn't mastered this intricate mechanism. All the signals are coming in normally on his screen, but he can't tell the difference between a squadron of jet planes and a flock of sparrows.

To me, that's what it's like to be a child—a fledgling operator at the controls of that miraculous machine we call a mind. The child sees what we see, and yet he doesn't—for he lacks the experience to interpret it properly. Driven on by his curiosity and eagerness to make sense of the world, he often creates a delightful kind of nonsense, an almost-sense, instead.

A signal flashes onto the child's screen. It's a question:

"What is the chief end of man?"

The boy replies:

"It's the end that the head sits on."

Everybody laughs, but the boy is right! I often hear wonderfully unexpected lines like that when a youngster is doing his best to reason things out. I call answers like this "skid talk," because they slide right past where you think they'll go, and end up somewhere else.

Here are more of my favorite sliders:

What does the expression, "Easy come, easy go," mean?
It means you have an automobile and you don't have to walk.

❖ ❖ ❖

Are you a pessimist?
No, I go to confession.

❖ ❖ ❖

What does "mother-in-law" mean?
No matter what happens or what anybody says, she's the law!

❖ ❖ ❖

What's the difference between alimony and matrimony?
Davy Crockett was shot in the Alimony, and Matt Dillon was shot in the Matrimony.

❖ ❖ ❖

Do you believe in matrimony?
Yes, if it has cheese on it.

There are dozens of common expressions in use by grown-ups which are just as bewildering to kids as they are to foreigners. A saying such as "I lost my head" sounds very curious indeed to a youngster who takes it literally. Let's see how the kids do in defining some familiar expressions:

What does it mean to "build castles in the air"?
It means you're going to fire a rocket up and put a space station between here and the moon.

❖   ❖   ❖

What's "a horse of another color"?
A zebra.

❖   ❖   ❖

How does a person "talk turkey"?
Gobble-gobble-gobble.

❖   ❖   ❖

What does "butter wouldn't melt in her mouth" mean?
A girl has a cold tongue.

❖   ❖   ❖

What does "burning the candle at both ends" mean?
Ouch!

❖   ❖   ❖

"Fingers in every pie"?
The guy's got some kind of job like a pie-taster.

❖   ❖   ❖

"Too many cooks spoil the broth"?
Nobody in the whole family can cook.

❖   ❖   ❖

"Have your cake and eat it too"?
Mama bought two cakes.

❖   ❖   ❖

What's the expression "cook your goose" mean?
Search me. I've never cooked one.

❖ ❖ ❖

What does "eat humble pie" mean?
It's not cooked; it's raw.

❖ ❖ ❖

What does it mean to "take the bull by the horns"?
If a bullfighter drops his sword, that's the only thing left for him to do!

Kids like these remind me of the little girl in the second grade who was signing up for the school's thrift program. She

did fine in filling out the form until she came to the space that asked her to "Name previous bank." After thinking carefully, she wrote "Piggy."

Confusion seems to reach new heights around election time. If the average voter thinks the politicians have him a

little groggy, he should listen to the school kids. I'm talking
to eleven-year-old Ronald:

"What's your favorite song?"
"The Battle Hymn of the Republicans."
"How can you tell the Republicans and Democrats
apart?"
"The Democrats have a mule sign—and the Republicans
are chickens."

❖   ❖   ❖

What's the difference between Democrats and Republicans?
One is real great for the country, but the other one's
just terrible!
Which is which?
That's the part I don't know.

❖   ❖   ❖

What was Martha Washington famous for?
She married Abraham Lincoln.

❖   ❖   ❖

What was the greatest thing that Lincoln ever did?
Beat the Germans.

❖   ❖   ❖

What was the greatest thing that Washington ever did?
He let the Indians go free.

My little history experts are just as vague about the whole
idea of time and its passage. We grown-ups literally live by
our sweep-second watches and split-second schedules, so it's

refreshing to see how incredibly elastic time can be in the minds of the young. Ask a small child to tell the difference between being young, middle-aged and old, and you'll hear replies like this:

❖ My sister is young; she's four. My brother is middle-aged; he's six. And my mother is old; she's twenty-one.

❖ Young is when you have bubble gum. When you're middle-aged, you're cleaning up after other people's gum. And if

you're old, you have false teeth and you better not chew any bubble gum.

❖ Young is when you're like me, running all over and there's not enough time to do everything. Old is like my dad, when all you do is eat and sleep because that's all there's time for. *How old is your dad?*

He must be at least thirty by now.

❖ When you're young, everybody blames you for everything. When you're middle-aged, you can blame some of the others, and when you're old, you blame everybody.

I asked a girl to tell me the meaning of the expression, "Time marches on," and she said:

"One day it's December 5 and before you know it, it's April 15, and you're supposed to pay your income taxes next day."

"But you're only seven," I said. "How do you know so much about income taxes?"

"My dad's the tax collector," she explained.

"Why do we have income taxes?"

"We've just *got* to!"

"But why?"

"To pay my dad's salary."

What do you think it means to say that time marches on?

❖ It's like when my mother sits down at three-thirty to read a Perry Mason story, and suddenly my father is home and there's nothing ready for his dinner yet."

❖ It's like my mother's age. She'll be thirty-two next month—and already she's baking a cake with twenty-nine candles on it.

❖   ❖   ❖

What is the worst age to be?

Twenty-one, because you have a lot of responsibility then. You have to take matters into your own hands, like dressing and maybe voting for the wrong man.

❖ ❖ ❖

Six-year-old Reuben just couldn't imagine *any* age when he'd face worse problems than he's having right now.

"What's the matter?"

"I don't like to go in the girls' bathroom."

"Then why do you do it?"

"My mother hauls me in there."

A ten-year-old girl had this "biggest worry":

"It's when I forget my lunch on cleaning day, and Mom comes to school with it in her old clothes and bandana, and the kids look at her and say, 'Is *that* your mother?' "

Another ten-year-old named Joan, wise beyond her years, was wrestling with a very practical problem:

"I don't know whether I should plug a store on your show and get myself a free transistor radio, or whether I would get my neck wrung by the government payola guys."

(Joan decided to skip the commercial, and as far as I know, she is still at large.)

The kids aren't the only worry warts I hear about. Many parents get the whoops and jingles at the mere thought of taking their offspring to dinner in a public place, for fear they'll act as they sometimes do at home—stuffing their mouths like hungry squirrels, blowing bubbles in the milk, and whooping like Iroquois Indians on a scalping raid. To avoid such disasters, every family has its rules.

What's an example of good manners?

Don't yell at the table.

Why not?

You might make the waiter nervous so he spills soup on you.

❖   ❖   ❖

What's your idea of good table manners?

When you're eating, never wipe your hands on your clothes.

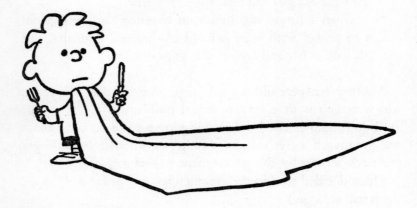

That's a good rule. What should you do instead?

Wipe them on the tablecloth.

Behavior when the kids stay home with a baby sitter can be a fascinating topic, too. Kids have very definite ideas on which sitters they like best, and how they should behave. I asked a pair of seven-year-olds to tell me about the baby sitters they preferred:

❖ I like young ones, because the old ones are crabby and get scared when you swing on the refrigerator door and it tips over.

❖ I like old ones, because the young ones just say, "Go away and don't bother me and my boy friend."

A recent survey on the television viewing habits of children revealed a rather startling statistic—that the average kid spends more time during the week watching tv than he does in school! I'll leave to you parents the wisdom of allowing so much televiewing by your boys and girls, and press on to what the kids themselves have to say about the family watching machine.

A panel of seven-year-olds named their favorite shows for me:

❖ I like the "Three Stooges" because they don't have any of that lovey, mushy stuff.
(Must I add that it was a boy who said that?)

❖ I like "Video Village" because it's like Monopoly come to life, and there's a lot of yelling and prizes.

❖ "National Velvet" is the best show, because it teaches you to sponge off your horse after riding.

❖ I like "Mickey Mouse" when I'm well, and when I'm sick I watch *you*, Mr. Linkletter!

The same group was asked what they do when the commercial comes on:

❖ Dad goes for the beer, Mom makes a ham sandwich, and I go to the bathroom.

❖ I stay and watch because they're the best part of the show.
(Sometimes they are!)

❖ I go see Grandpa. He lives a block away, and by then the show is back on.

❖ I just sit there and suffer through them.

All sponsors of tv shows who survived the previous paragraph will now mercifully shut their eyes, because the next paragraph will only disillusion them completely.

I asked a group of ten-year-olds to tell me the principal purpose of tv commercials. Here's how they answered:

❖ To tell the people how cheap the sponsors are.

❖ To give the stars time to look over their scripts so they won't forget their parts.

❖ To stop the show in the interesting part so you don't know when the interesting stuff starts again.

❖ To give everybody time to get something from the icebox.

❖ ❖ ❖

What's a "private eye"?

He's a private policeman who looks out the corner of his eye without letting the crooks know he's watching them.

❖ ❖ ❖

What's an "Emmy"?

It's a bad guy who shoots you from behind when you're not looking.

Oh, sure, that's right. Everybody has friends and emmys.

❖ ❖ ❖

How does color television work?

They have a little man living inside with a paint brush,

and as fast as he hears on his little telephone what the picture is supposed to be, he paints it.

That's exactly what I always thought.

Marco Polo learned in his travels that the Chinese of his day believed they lived at the exact center of the universe. Nowadays, of course, we know better: the center of the universe is in Texas. But I met a boy the other day who was unaware of this, and thought there was nothing so fine in all the world as Staten Island. So I asked him:

"New York Harbor is famous for something that everybody looks for when they come to this country. Can you tell me what this is?"

"Well, I know you can get four sticks of licorice for a penny there. You only get one in Los Angeles."

"But what about the Statue of Liberty? Isn't that kind of famous, too?"

"Oh, sure. It's around there."

Let's see what happens when we talk about money:

If you found a ten dollar bill and wanted to surprise your folks with a gift, what would you buy?

❖ I'd buy them both some pajamas. They don't wear any.

❖ I'd give the money to my dad to play golf, so he could walk right out on the first tee, instead of sneaking in on the third or fourth!

CHAPTER XV

A Child's Garden
of Daydreams

IMAGINATION is the natural gift of poets, writers, artists, musicians—and the very young. Little children are blessed with minds that soar up and away on the lightest fancy. As one writer said, the gates of paradise have not yet closed behind them.

After years of interviewing hundreds of children, I know how fragile a thing imagination can be. It must be encouraged to show itself, to come out into the open, or you will never know it's there. But once you win the confidence of a child, he will open his heart and tell you the wonderful, magical things inside.

Imagination lasts no longer than a rainbow in the harsh light of reality. Tell a child often enough that he is talking nonsense, or ought to know better, and the rainbow will fade away. I've gone the other way with my children, knowing the facts will catch up with them soon enough. To me, there's no game so fine in all the world for children as "Let's Pretend."

Here is one little imagination at work making gossamer things, deftly weaving facts and fancy into one skein:

"Tommy, what makes it cold?"

"The deep freeze in heaven is left open overnight."

"Freddy, if you could have three wishes, what would they be?"

"A space helmet, a spaceship, and a brother."

"Why do you want the spaceship?"

"To go to the moon."

"What do you suppose you'd see there?"

"Moon animals, like the moon cow."

"How would you milk a moon cow?"

"It's hard to do, because there's gravity and you would have to milk it upside down, so the spigots would have to be up, and you down, and the cow, too, and sometimes it would squirt in your eye!"

I've always enjoyed Mexican food, but I can no longer order one South-of-the-border dish without remembering this conversation with an imaginative youngster:

"What do you like to eat best?"

"Enchiladas."

"How do you make one?"

"First you have to catch them."

"Catch them? Do you know what they look like?"

"They're round and have eight legs."

"How do you cook them?"

"You just put them in the oven and bake them till they don't kick no more."

"You've just ruined one of my favorite dishes for me."

I've never seen a mermaid, but a boy on my show was convinced that *he* had.

"What have you been doing lately?"

"I went to Disneyland and went on the submarine ride."

"What did you see?"

"A real mermaid."

"What did she look like?"

"Just a regular girl, except she didn't have a seat—just a tail."

Some kids are so imaginative that their mental reflexes act like computers. Wild ideas bob up in their heads as fast as I can ask the questions. Here's a memorable exchange I had with a kindergartener whose imagination ran wide open all the time:

"What's your favorite time of the year?"

"Easter. You can find more eggs then."

"How do you suppose the Easter Bunny gets so many eggs?"

"He steals them from a hen."

"What does the Bunny look like?"

"Like a sleeve off a big fur coat, with a big white mustache."

"How does he stay so white all year long?"

"He takes bubble baths."

"You don't have much of an imagination, do you?"

"I haven't noticed one."

"You must be pretty smart at kindergarten."

"I'm only five and I can spell."

"All right—spell 'cow.' "

"C-O-W."

"Now spell my name, 'Art.' "

"R-A-T."

"Let's get on to something else. What's the best part of kindergarten?"

"Writing."

"What's the worst part?"

"No fighting, no biting, no pushing, no cheating, no throwing sand in anybody's eyes, and no throwing paint."

"It must be pretty dull if you can't do those things. But what's the very worst part about it all?"

"You have to take turns."

Here are some more gems from the wonderful imaginations of our flourishing younger generation:

What's a "conscience"?

It's a gray ghost inside of you with a friendly face, but it stops smiling when your nerves begin to write a note to it when you want to do something bad, and when the ghost gets this bad note he gets very angry and yells "Stop!"

I see. How did you get so smart?

We have a whole set of encyclopedias at home.

What's an encyclopedia?

I don't know; I can't read.

❖ ❖ ❖

The same question about "conscience" brought this appealing definition from a six-year-old girl:

"Conscience is an angel in your heart."

❖ ❖ ❖

Many a grownup would struggle with the task of defining a word like "imagination," but a little boy did it beautifully with this sentence:

"Imagination is running away from yourself in your mind."

❖ ❖ ❖

When you meet a child with a vivid imagination, you hear tales so tall that they make Liar's Club members sound like gospel singers. I knew I had an imaginer the moment I asked a six-year-old if he had a secret.

"Yes," he said leaning forward very confidentially. "There are a couple of dinosaurs and a thunder lizard in the audience."

"How would they get in here past the ushers?"

"They change themselves into people just outside the building."

"That's quite a story! Do you have any more?"

"My mother and dad were Chinamen, and after they got married, they turned into Americans."

"You have quite a mind. What do you want to be when you grow up?"

"I'm going to be a bone collector."

"What kind of bones? Dinosaur bones?"

"No, I like to collect snail bones!"

❖ ❖ ❖

Another tall-tale teller was Charles, aged five, who told me what had happened just the other day:

"I went to Grandma's," he said, "and there was a giraffe in her bed and he was eating her lamp."

"You dreamed this?"

"NO! I was *there!* And before I could run out of the room, the giraffe ate me up!"

"Well, you're here, so you must have escaped. How did you do that?"

"I got out by using his bones for a ladder."

❖ ❖ ❖

Another boy with a wild-blue-yonder mind told a whopper when I asked him to describe the funniest thing he'd ever seen:

"Yesterday I heard a rap on the back door," he began, "and when I opened it, this funny thing was there."

"What 'funny thing'?"

"Well, it had the feet of a horse and the neck of a lion, and the body of a cow and a tail like a fish."

"What did you do with it?"

"I brought it in and introduced it to my dog."

"What did your dog do?"

"He ran out of the house, and I haven't seen him since."

"I don't blame him! Where is this 'thing' now?"

"Oh, it's home, watching us on television."

A favorite fantasy of most humans, young and old, is the dream of Aladdin's lamp, with its fulfillment of any wish we have. Children around five are especially fond of the "three wishes" game.

If you could have three wishes, what would they be?

❖ A new car I didn't have to pay for, to be king of the world so I could stop everybody from fighting, and to have special shoes with the socks glued in so I could jump into both of them at once.

❖ To be an angel, a plain old fairy, and a tooth fairy.

❖ To be a princess, to be a bird, and to have a church of my own where I could pray for everybody.

Like most fathers, it's the little girls who make my heart flip-flop with their sweet, trusting replies. Who could deny that "God's in his Heaven, and all's right with the world" when he hears a five-year-old talk about what she's going to wish for on her next "birfday."

"I want to go to the moon and wave to my mommy and daddy."

"And how do you think you'll get to the moon?"

"On angel's wings."

"But what would you do if you found that you couldn't get back to earth?"

"I'd call God on the phone and say, 'Help!'"

What age would you say we live in—the Automotive Age? The Nuclear Age? The Electronic Age? Sorry, but all three are wrong.

I asked a boy what age he'd choose to live in, and he told me:

"Right now! The Cowboy Age."

"It is? Well, all right then. But why is this such a good Age?"

"Because you can get a job on any channel."

Oh, how right he is!

One way to set imaginations going is to make kids search their minds for answers, like this:

"What do you think is the hardest job in the world?"

(Shirley, 7) "Being a successful bank robber."

(Dustin, 6) "Being an electrician, because it's so hard to make electricity."

(Richard, 7) "Being a husband."

Every woman in the audience must have felt a heart tug for six-year-old Michael when I asked him who he'd like to marry.

He thought very carefully, and then soberly replied:
"A mother."

It's fun to toss a fantastic situation at a child, and see what
he flings back at you. Here are a few fast ones:

*Gary, what if you found out you were the world's richest
man?*
First I'd faint. Then I'd buy a bowling alley.

❖   ❖   ❖

*Morrie, what if you were a lifeguard and saw someone
drowning?*

He'd just have to drown. I can't swim!

❖   ❖   ❖

*Stevie, what if you saw a hungry lion coming down the
street, and he wanted to eat you?*
I'd say, "Get away, I'm not cooked!"

❖ ❖ ❖

Jerry, what if you could change places with a famous President; who would you be?
Abraham Lincoln.
What would you do differently?
Instead of going to that opera, I'd stay home and watch Art Linkletter.

❖ ❖ ❖

Donna, you're only six. But what would you do if you were the President's wife?
I'd have a big party and invite George.
George who?
George Washington.

❖ ❖ ❖

Martin, you're five. Can you tell me how people walk?
Yes. Your bones move and your skin just follows.

❖ ❖ ❖

Joe, what's the ugliest thing you've ever seen?
A squashed skunk.

❖ ❖ ❖

What is "magic"?
A man says, "Aba-ca-daba"—and then pulls an elephant out of his hat.
I'd like to see that stunt myself!

❖ ❖ ❖

Have you done anything interesting lately?
Yesterday I had a funeral for my poor old pet toad.

Did you have a tombstone and write anything on it?

Yes. It said, "Here lies my toad. He was my best toad and he loved me but my dad stepped on him."

When December rolls around, I always find that all the younger boys and girls are wriggling with curiosity about Santa Claus. A kid may not know our President from the Emperor of Japan, but he has a complete file in his head on Santa.

"Sherry, how does Santa Claus know if you're good all year long?"

"He has spies."

"He has? What kind?"

"Russian. What other kind is there?"

Jimmy is a six-year-old who's just beginning to notice certain curious coincidences around Christmas time. But he's fighting to keep his illusions.

"Jimmy, why does Santa wear a red suit?"

"So everyone won't think he's my daddy."

Here's one of the most charming flights of whimsy I've ever heard. The more you think about it, the more enchanting a picture it forms in your mind:

"What's your biggest wish?"

"I'd like to change the name of our school to Santa Claus School."

"Why is that?"

"I think it would be a lot of fun if Santa Claus was our teacher."

Ah, what a classroom that would be!

Ten-year-old Roger told me he'd much rather be President than the King of England.

"Why?"

"Because I hate tea."

It's a national pastime to second-guess the President, and people follow the weekly polls on his popularity the way we used to follow our favorite baseball players. Be happy, then, that none of these youngsters is in the White House, after hearing what they'd do if they were President:

❖ I'd paint the White House red, white and blue.

❖ I'd have fifty children—one for each state.

❖ I'd just put my feet up on the desk and relax.

❖ I'd head for Las Vegas. Boy, I bet you'd have plenty of money to work the slot machines!

Everybody daydreams once in a while about what he'd do if he had all the money he could wish for. Here are two intriguing ideas for spending a million dollars.

❖ First I'd buy a hot rod, then an air rifle, and if I had any money left over, I'd buy a wife.

❖ I'd buy our school, and let all the little boys and girls go free.

Sleep is a subject that has baffled our greatest scientists. It doesn't bother the kids a bit.

Here's a quick roundup of four youngsters' ideas about where they go when they go to sleep:

Kathleen: "I go to Grandma's."

Deborah: "I go to the moon."

Ralph: "I go to heaven."

Charlie: "I go out."

"Out where?"

"Out cold!"

"What do you think life will be like on this planet a thousand years from now?" I asked a young science-minded boy who promptly predicted:

"There won't be many people left."

"Why not?"

"They will be living on different planets."

"Then you think that people on earth will be *extinct?*"

"Oh, no. They'll still have to take baths."

❖   ❖   ❖

Many a hero has been decorated for bravery when the underlying motivation for the act was less than heroic.

Here's a preview:

"What do you want to be, Reuben?"

"A fireman."

"Suppose CBS caught fire this very moment. Who would you rescue?"

"You."

"Why me?"

" 'Cause you haven't given me my prize yet."

❖   ❖   ❖

How would you spend a perfect day? Before your answer limits your fun, listen to ten-year-old Mark's idea:

"I'd go to Hawaii, get sick, and hire a hula dancer as my nurse."

❖   ❖   ❖

And here's a wish we've all had on Thanksgiving Day, perfectly and succinctly expressed by an eight-year-old:

"I'd wish for a turkey with sixteen drumsticks."

Time was when the thought of having to entertain a hungry mob at dinner would make almost anyone quail. But ours is a modern age, and four grade-school kids dealt with the problem quite handily when I asked what they'd do for twenty-five hungry guests:

❖ I'd just thaw out some cheap tv dinners.

❖ I'd fix twenty-five fried eggs.

❖ I'd just call the caterer.

❖ I'd tell them to bring their own!

Kids and tv sets seem to go together like book-ends, so I was quite startled when one young man announced he'd like to sell the family tv set.
"Why?"
"I hate the commercials."
"Mine, too?"
"Well . . . are you going to give us some toys?"

Another boy had a heartfelt wish to sell something around his house:
"My brother, that's what I'd sell—if my mom wasn't looking."

Certain smells, fragrances and aromas have the power to evoke vivid memories of the past. They can be anything from the sweetness of new-mown hay to a bar of soap with a special scent. I know what smells will always be remembered by a certain group of six-year-olds, because I asked them for their favorites. Here they are:
"A Christmas Tree."
"A rose."
"Tacos."
"My mother."

Ask a child what famous parents he'd like to have, and the answer may startle you, as five-year-old Skippy did me recently, when he said:
"I'd like my parents to be Art Linkletter and Red Skelton."

"Hey, wait a minute. We're both boys."

"That's okay. You can be the mother."

My son Jack's name popped up when I asked a ten-year-old girl what famous husband she'd like. When I asked why she picked Jack, she looked me right in the eye and said:

"Because he's funny, cute, and younger than you."

Five-year-old Tony picked an odd pair for his imaginary parents—George Washington and Shirley Temple.

"Why?"

"Because George was our country's father, and I think Shirley would be a swell mother if she had a chance!"

He's right, too! She did. She was. And she still is.

Someone once told me that the United States, early in its history, came within one vote of choosing German instead of English as our national language. Imagine how that would have changed the events of the past two hundred years!

I often ask the kids how they'd change history, and the answers I get go like this:

❖ I'd like to have Benedict Arnold be President of the United States.

Why Arnold, of all people?

I'd like to see one of the bad guys win once in a while!

❖ I'd fix it so there were no murders, no narcotics, and no school.

❖ I'd see to it that America would never be discovered and we wouldn't have to read about it.

❖ I'd like to have Abe Lincoln faster on the draw than John Wilkes Booth.

So would I!

CHAPTER XVI

Whippersnapper Snappers

Do you remember that old-fashioned carnival game where you threw baseballs at a target, hoping to score a bull's-eye that would trip a lever and send a clown tumbling down into a huge tub of water? Sometimes I feel like that clown as the four school kids line up each day to take turns at me. Sooner or later, I know, one of them will say something right "on target" and drop me into a tub of laughter. And there are many days, I'm happy to say, when I'm thoroughly dunked!

Here are some of the pitches, straight and fast, that have knocked me off my perch:

"What's the biggest problem in growing up?"
"Amnesia."
"Do you know what 'amnesia' is?"
"You take a spoonful in a glass of water."

❖   ❖   ❖

"What do you think is the problem age?"
"My age—eleven."
"Why?"

"Because you're too young to date, and too old to believe in Santa Claus."

❖ ❖ ❖

"Shirley, how does a six-year-old like you help her mother?"

"I help change my baby sister."

"How do you do that?"
"Carefully."

All comedians know that laughter depends upon the surprising and the unexpected. A professional funny man deliberately leads you in a certain direction—and then pulls the rug out from under you. Kids are natural comics because they do the same thing. The difference is that kids don't do this intentionally. They get their laughs without even trying!

Here are some rug-pullers in action:

"What *wouldn't* you want to be?"
"A nun."
"Why not?"
"Because I'm Jewish."

❖ ❖ ❖

"Gary, can a five-year-old like you tell time?"
"I'm learning to."
"What time is it now?"
"Daytime."

❖ ❖ ❖

"What do we mean by the saying, 'Time flies'?"
"It's when you're up in an airplane with a watch on."

❖ ❖ ❖

"Do you know which animals got aboard Noah's ark?"
"Yes, the lucky ones."

❖ ❖ ❖

"Johnny, you're old enough to read the newspapers. What is a recession?"
"It's something you have after a wedding."
(After marrying off two members of the Linkletter family, I think the boy is right!)

Here are some more surprisers that listeners have sent me:

A four-year-old girl notices the tag on a dog's collar and asks what it is.
"It's his license," says the man.
"Oh," says the girl. "Does he drive?"

❖ ❖ ❖

A little boy is trudging down the path with his fishing pole on Sunday morning. The minister sees him and asks:
"Son, do you know where little boys go when they fish on Sunday?"
"Sure! Follow me and I'll show you."

❖ ❖ ❖

A six-year-old comes home with a new ball.
"Where did you get that?" asks his mother.
"George gave it to me for doing him a favor."
"What favor?"
"I was hitting him on the back and he asked me to stop."

❖ ❖ ❖

Two little boys are eating ice cream and one drops a scoop on the back of a woman's mink coat.
"Be careful!" says his friend. "You're getting fur all over your ice cream!"

Besides being surprising, a good joke is brief and straight to the point. This is why comics are fond of the so-called "one-liners" that are told in a single statement. Kids are masters of one-liners. I call them "whippersnapper snappers" and they sound like this:

What do you think the biggest change in 1962 will be?
It won't be 1961 anymore.

❖ ❖ ❖

What's the first thing you'd do if you were elected President of the United States?
Resign.

❖ ❖ ❖

So you want to be a fireman. What's the first thing a fireman needs?
A fire.

❖ ❖ ❖

How do giraffes look?
With their eyeballs.

❖ ❖ ❖

How do you tell if somebody is a good friend?
He's a good friend if he doesn't blab when you sock him in the nose.

Speaking of surprisers, a little girl startled me not long ago by telling me that the hot place where many people go is *heaven.*

"What makes you think heaven is a hot place?" I asked.

"It must be," she said. "All they wear up there is wings and a halo."

CHAPTER XVII

Out on a Limb
of the Family Tree

WHEN *Kids Say the Darndest Things* was published, Jack Benny wrote this delightful comment:

"Some people wonder if these kids really think up the things they say to Art, but I know they do. I hate to tell any secrets about Art's age, but when I was a kid, I was on the show and I had to furnish all my own material."

The truth is that children are natural comics. They seldom waste a word in telling you an experience, and as Shakespeare said, "Brevity is the soul of wit." Kids have an instinct for a punchline—that totally unexpected reaction that derails your logic and starts you laughing.

Here are a few choice exchanges with small fry comics:

Richard, what's your dad's biggest problem?
  Tequila.
Your father drinks?
  No, Tequila's our dog.

❖ ❖ ❖

How did your folks meet, Christopher?
My aunt found my daddy for my mom in a cookie shop.
I suppose your mommy calls him "Cookie"?
No, she calls him "crumb."

❖ ❖ ❖

Jeff, who would you like to be if you were somebody famous?
Eddie Fisher.
Do you like his voice?
No, I like his wife.

❖ ❖ ❖

Judith, you're eleven years old. What's your main problem at school dances?
Short boys with icy hands.

Every happy family seems to have its private jokes, those funny and sometimes racy explanations of how the parents supposedly met, or fell in love. The catch is that their trusting offspring hear these gags around the house, and take them for gospel truth. And then, when the kid blurts it out on my show, the gag is on Mom and Dad.

Bobby, how did your folks meet and get married?
Ha, ha, that's funny. They aren't even married!

❖ ❖ ❖

Jimmy, how did your folks meet?
They were both poor, but my mom owned a bath and my dad wanted to share it with her.

❖ ❖ ❖

Charlotte?
Dad drove a milk truck and Mom was waiting, sitting on a bottle.

❖ ❖ ❖

Ronnie?
It was kind of exciting. They were both Marines in the war. Mom was in the top bunk and Dad was in the bottom bunk and they kept running into each other when they got up in the morning.

The simple truth can often cause just as much consternation when repeated as any family joke. Imagine how a certain dignified, briefcase-carrying gentleman of the law must have felt when I asked his son:

What does your dad do?
He's a lawyer for CBS.
What's the hardest part of his job?
Getting his pay from CBS.

❖ ❖ ❖

Here's another:
What does your daddy do?
    He's a doctor.
What's the hardest thing a doctor does?
    Giving people a hernia.

❖ ❖ ❖

What do your mother and dad do?
    Dad's a minister and Mom's a housewife.
What does your dad do for fun?
    He rings the church bell.

And your mom?
    I don't know. She's expecting.

❖ ❖ ❖

What do your mom and dad do?

Dad's a Shakespearian actor and she's a Shakespearian actress.

What's their favorite play?

The Taming of the Shrew. They practice it all the time at home.

Why do they like it?

Because people knock each other all over the place.

How did your folks meet?

They were in the illegitimate theater.

❖ ❖ ❖

What's your dad?

A mechanic.

What does your mother do?

Nothing special.

How many brothers and sisters do you have?

Ten brothers and seven sisters.

And your mother does "nothing special"?

No, she just lays around the house.

I don't blame her!

❖ ❖ ❖

What does your dad do?

He's a waiter on a train.

How does he like it?

Fine, except that once in a while he gets mad.

When is that?

When the train leaves without him.

❖ ❖ ❖

What's your dad?

A preacher.

What kind of church?
   A pink one with a blue roof.

❖   ❖   ❖

What does your dad do?
   He's a dry cleaner.
Can you tell me who's President of the United States?
   Abraham Lincoln.
Where does he live?
   I don't know; we never pick up any of his clothes.

❖   ❖   ❖

What does your father do?
   He's a Congressman in Washington, D.C.
What do you think it's like in Washington?
   George Washington rides up and down there, watching
to see that nobody chops down the trees.

❖   ❖   ❖

Is your dad handy around the house?
   He sure is.
What did he ever fix?
   My mother's back.

Parents usually enjoy a joke on themselves as much as the
audience does. Naturally Dad laughs the loudest when Mother
is the butt of the joke, and vice versa. But sometimes a child

launches a shaft with such deadly accuracy that it brings a yelp from the parent that can literally be heard from coast to coast, like this:

"Would you describe your mother?"

"Well, she used to have blonde hair but she's dyed it red so often that it's falling out."

At this point a muffled shriek came from a redheaded woman in the audience. I said:

"What was *that?*"

"I guess it was my mom. She always yells when I say things like that."

One of the surest ways to get a glimpse of a child's family life is to ask him who's boss around the house. We Americans have evidently gone a long way from the Victorian era when father was absolute master of the manse. Judging by the testimony of thousands of school kids, Dad now divides his authority with Mom. Some households still operate the old-fashioned way, with Dad issuing rules from on high, and in some homes it has gone to the opposite extreme, with Mom taking complete charge.

I like the story about the husband who told a friend, "I make all the big decisions in our family, and my wife handles the little ones." His friend asked what he meant, and he told him: "I decide what we think about atomic energy, disarmament, and things like that, and my wife decides where we'll live, the kind of car we'll drive and what we'll do with the paycheck each week!"

Let's see how dear old Dad is doing:

"Who's the boss in your family?"

"My dad."

"Why do you think so?"

"The only reason I can figure out is that he sits at the head of the table at dinner."

Actor Lloyd "Sea Hunt" Bridges is a fearless hero to millions, and a devoted family man at home. I asked his daughter Sandy: "Who's boss around your house?"

"Daddy's the boss in the movies, and Mom's boss at home."

Another girl told me her dad was an officer in the Marine Corps. I asked her: "What's his rank?"

"What's that mean?"

"How important is he?"

"I don't know. Around our house, Mom is boss."

"Who's boss in your family?"

"Dad. He won't wear the shorts my mom buys for him because they're too tight."

"Then what happens?"

"She gives them to my uncle. He doesn't like 'em either."

"Is there an end to this story?"

"Yes. My aunt wears them."

Everybody loves to see dignity get a good swift kick in the pants. It's a joyful feeling that persists from childhood, when we were helpless little beings under the domination of others. What fun it was to see those big pompous adults come a cropper once in a while!

The fun of seeing dignity and authority brought low often comes when I'm talking to kids about their fathers. An audience with problems of its own will rock with laughter at the exposure of an expert's own difficulties:

Where does your daddy work, Andy?
  In a marriage clinic.
What upsets a marriage counselor?
  Mom's yelling.
Who's she yelling at?
  Dad.

❖ ❖ ❖

Have you ever wondered how the financial wizards do
with their own family budgets? Listen to this:

What's your dad, Steve?
  A banker.
What's your family like?
  Just average.
What do you mean "average"?
  We owe everybody.

❖ ❖ ❖

Ten-year-old Judy gave us all a shock when I asked what
her daddy did.
  He's in the burglary business.
You mean he robs houses?
  No, he owns the United States Burglar Alarm Company.
How's business?
  Wonderful. There are more robberies than he can handle!

❖ ❖ ❖

What's your dad do, Brenda?
  He has an unusual kind of job. He works in a dry cleaning plant taking lipstick marks out of men's collars.

❖ ❖ ❖

How about your dad?
  He's a policeman.
What's his biggest problem?
  Women drivers.
Who's the best driver in your family?
  My mom.

Modern writers have been taking us Americans to task lately for becoming a nation of "status seekers." They say that we're spending our lives in one great feverish scramble for symbols of prestige—those jobs, homes and cars that will impress our friends and neighbors. Kids are blissfully unaware of this drive to look better than we are. In fact they have a delightfully perverse way of putting the family's worst foot forward.

"Karen, what's your family like?"
"My dad's fat, my grandmother's fat, I guess my dog has the best shape of anybody."

"Phyllis, what about your family?"

"Dad's the youngest, my mom's the oldest and no matter *what* my dad says to my mother, she never goes home to her mother!"

"Gwendolyn, you're five now. Who's the smartest person you know in your family?"

"Nobody's very smart in my family."

Kids show the same refreshing frankness in appraising themselves as they do others:

Describe yourself.

I'm un-normal for a boy. I don't like football or westerns, and I read a lot.

What do you plan to be?

A criminal lawyer like Daniel Webster. I want to prove that people are not guilty.

Would you take a case if the man were guilty and you knew it?

Not in a thousand years—unless I needed the money!

❖ ❖ ❖

What are you like, young lady?
    Nothing about me's false.
What do you mean?
    I don't have any false eyelashes, false teeth or false hair, and I don't wear any falsies.

❖ ❖ ❖

What are you like, Herbert?
    I'm goodhearted.
Give me an example.
    I give my sister half ownership in anything that she pays half on.

❖ ❖ ❖

Describe yourself in a sentence:
❖ My name is Carol, my age is eight, and I'm sixty-eight pounds of blubber.
❖ My name is Kurt, my age is ten, and I'm sexy, boy, that's all.
❖ I'm just one-half Jewish and one whole Christian.

The school kids have enlightened me on all sorts of odd topics and stray facts down through the years. What they tell me may not always be gospel, but it's sure to be interesting. Did you know, for example, that good table manners began in the Garden of Eden? Neither did I, until I asked ten-year-old Jackie to give me an example of good manners.
    "Always put your napkin in your lap," she said.
    "Who started that custom?"

"Eve did."

"The first woman?"

"Yes."

"Why did she start it?"

"Because her lap seemed to be a good place to put her fig leaf."

Little Dennis told me one of the most important things to remember about good manners is to "always say your prayers before you eat."

"What do you pray?" I asked.

"I pray, 'Now I lay me down to eat'—but I can't remember the rest."

Dennis reminded me of the little girl who was saying grace in the bathtub when her mother heard her and said, "Darling, we only say grace when we're eating."

"I know it," said the girl. "I just swallowed the soap."

A girl with three brothers and four sisters revealed what good manners are in a family as large as hers:

"Don't run around eating, don't yell, and don't leave the toilet seat up."

Seven-year-old Karen told me she had a big family including five brothers and five sisters. I asked her what the rules might be in a herd like that, and she said:

"First my mother gets up in the morning and goes to the bathroom, and when she gets out she wakes my sister and *she* goes to the bathroom, then she wakes another sister and *she* goes to the bathroom, then my sister wakes my brother and he goes to the . . ."

"Wait!" I said. "We get the idea."

Little Maggie Slattery, the daughter of my announcer, Jack Slattery, told me their dinner-table rule:

"Keep your hands in your lap while you're eating."

Seven-year-old Richard obviously comes from a thrifty—and shifty—kind of family. I asked him:

"Are there any rules in your family?"

"One important one," he said. "If you make a phone call, always reverse the charges."

Whatever else kids are, they're not sophisticates about humor. They like clowns and slapstick because there's plenty of action, and they can *see* the joke happen. I've had many a laugh myself by asking the kids to tell me the funniest sights they've ever seen:

❖ My dad started to open a bottle of beer, and the top flew up and hit him in one eye, and the beer squirted in his other eye.

❖ My mom tried on all her underpants and they were too small, so she tried on Daddy's and they didn't fit either.

❖ My dad tried on his old Navy suit, and he couldn't button it around his tummy.

❖ My mother was getting into her girdle and she looked like a wriggly old snake. But when she finished, she looked real good.

❖ My mother wearing my dad's pajamas so he has to go to bed without them.

❖ My little brother playing with the dog when the dog bit him. Then my brother bit the dog back and he ran out of the house yelping.
Your brother?
No, the dog.

Now and then I run across a kid who's a real hipster, a breezy-tongued character who livens up a conversation with jazzy slang. Such a boy was crew-cut, eleven-year-old Mark, who gave this version of how his folks met:

"My mom was going around with a guy who had a cat boat, and then my dad came along. He was one of those guys who like to drive around and whistle at girls, and when my mom saw him in his red T-bird and heard that whistle, she let the guy with the cat boat go."

Here are more "How Mom Met Dad" stories, real and otherwise:

❖ Mother was a waitress and Dad came into the restaurant. *Did he tip her?*

I don't think so. He doesn't even wear a hat!

❖ My mom worked in a real estate office, and Dad was going to buy a bum house filled with termites. She tipped him off and Dad was so grateful he married her.

❖ My dad was walking down this street and he fainted, and my mother came along and dragged him into a drugstore. Then Dad said the only way he could pay her back was to drag her to the altar.

❖ My dad was in the Navy, and Mom was always there when the ship came in, to help with the anchor.

❖ My mom was a redhead and my dad liked them. He was a doctor and Mom wanted a free operation, so they got married, Mother had her appendix out, and Dad got a redhead—me.

❖ I don't know how they met—but I'm sure glad they did!

❖ My folks met on a wagon train. My daddy saved my mom from the Indians.

What's the main family rule at your house?
Don't fib.

What's the most fun at your house?
In the morning when I pull down my dad's pants while he's shaving.

Guadalupe was a pretty little Spanish girl of seven, with black eyes and a bright smile. I asked her how her folks met, and she said:

"My dad used to say the Rosary so slow that by the time he finished, my mother would be all through and on her way out of church. He wanted to meet her so much that he kept practicing until he could say it so fast that one day he finished quicker, and he caught up with her on the way out."

"And then what?"

"Here I am."

❖ ❖ ❖

Robert, how did your folks meet?

My mother was working in a grocery store and my dad came in to buy some eggs, but the minute he saw her, his heart turned around and around.

Then what?

He forgot about the eggs, but not about her.

❖ ❖ ❖

How did your folks meet?

Dad went to this dance by himself and he saw this wallflower so he went over and asked her to dance.

Do you know what a wallflower is?

Sure. It's a pretty lady standing by a wall.

That's not exactly it. Who told you she was a wallflower?

My mom.

Well, I guess that gets your dad off the hook!

❖ ❖ ❖

How did your folks get together?

Dad was the boss and Mom worked for him. She finally got tired of taking orders, so she married him—and now she gives the orders.

❖ ❖ ❖

How did your folks meet?

It happened at a picnic and Dad kept asking Mom to marry him, but she waited ten years.

What took her so long to say yes?
   She didn't want to act eager.

❖   ❖   ❖

How did your folks meet?
   Mom was at a dance and Dad paid her a dime to dance
with him, so they fell in love and got married.
That's a likely story. When did this happen?
   When I was three.

Dad isn't the only one in many modern families who brings
home problems from the office. Here's a peek into the life of
a working mom who's really busy.
   "My mom works at a big aircraft company."
   "Does she ever get upset?"
   "She sure does—the boss is always keeping her on the go."
   "What do you mean?"
   "He keeps chasing her around the desk."

❖   ❖   ❖

What does your mother look like?
   She's five feet two with eyes of blue and just twenty-two.
Who taught you to say that?
   My mother.
Is it true?
   Nope. She's really thirty-five.

❖   ❖   ❖

Who is the most beautiful woman in the world?
❖ My mom used to be, but now she's thirty-six and that's all
   finished.

❖ My mom, because if I don't say so, she'll bop me.

❖   ❖   ❖

I recognized many American families, including the Linkletters, when I heard the answer to this question:
Karen, what do your folks do for fun?
    Mostly they eat, and then mostly they diet.

❖   ❖   ❖

What's the most fun at your house?

❖ Dad puts ice cubes down my mom's back in bed.

❖ Dad pinches mommy on the fanny when she's cooking.
    What does your mom do?
    Pinches him right back!

❖ My dad likes to tell about the time Mom lost her swim-
    ing suit in the pool.

What does your mother do then?
    Hits him with a shoe.

❖   ❖   ❖

    My daddy likes to make signs.
    What do they say?

One says, "Don't just sit there—worry!" The other signs say "Men" and "Women."

❖   ❖   ❖

What's your idea of a good wife?
My mother.
Why?
Because she's always willing.
How do you know?
Because I have seven brothers and two sisters.

❖   ❖   ❖

Any secrets at your house?
Mom and Dad are celebrating their tenth anniversary.
What's so secret about that?
I don't know, but Daddy whispered to me that it seemed like ten decades. What's a decade, Mr. Linkletter?
Mommy will explain it to you both when you get home!

❧ CHAPTER XVIII ❧

Echoes From the Playpen

ONE of nature's recurring miracles happened in the Linkletter household recently. At the age of twenty-six months, my
grandson Michael said his first words. And as I looked down
at him in his playpen, I seemed to hear echoes of his father
Jack making his own first lisping efforts to communicate. I
wondered how soon this little boy, the first-born of my own
first-born, would be saying things like "elefunk" and "I wike
to eat breksaf" as his daddy did long ago. The wheel had come
full circle; the mystery and delight of a tiny human life had
begun all over again.

Listening to Mike took me back to the start of my career

190

on radio, when I first discovered that kids say the darndest things. With all the extravagant pride of a typical father, I had recorded Jack's bright sayings around home, and then played them over the air for my listeners. The reaction caught me by surprise. My mail was suddenly heavy with requests for more "kid talk." And so, without quite realizing what was happening, I was launched into a lifetime of fun and laughter with thousands and thousands of wonderful kids.

Although the world has changed almost unbelievably in our times, kids are still the same at heart as they always were. When I was a boy, the wonder of our lives was the marvelous tin Lizzie that raced down our streets at forty breakneck miles an hour.

Today's kid gets the same kick out of the latest be-chromed and superpowered autos that can streak along at a hundred miles an hour. Kids of my day thrilled to the screen gunfights of Tom Mix in the same way that today's boys and girls enjoy the cowboys on tv. Yesterday's kids wanted to be like Charles Lindbergh, who flew alone across the vast Atlantic in a tiny single-engined biplane. It's hardly surprising that today's boy wants to be like another Lone Eagle, Commander Alan B. Shepard, our first hero in space. Life has become so different, but kids will always be kids, with the same eager yearnings for adventure and knowledge.

This book was never intended to carry a "message." My only wish has been to make you laugh, and maybe, along the way to remind you of the merry times I hope you had during your own childhood and, if you're a parent, with your own kids. But if there were a message to be given, it would be something like writer Harry Golden's famous expression, "Enjoy, enjoy!" Through the years, I've met many well-meaning parents who were so conscientious and so weighed down by the responsibilities of parenthood that they couldn't *enjoy* their kids. I certainly won't deny that being a mother or dad is the most serious job in life. But there's fun in it, too! Kids are amazingly resilient, durable creatures. They turn out just fine with enough love and kisses to grow on. So I say, relax and enjoy them. And be sure to talk *with* them often, because —kids still say the darndest things!